SUPPLY-SIDE STEWARDSHIP

SUPPLY-SIDE STEWARDSHIP

A Call to Biblical Priorities

Waldo J. Werning

Publishing House
St. Louis

3558 South Jefferson Avenue, St. Louis, MO 63118-3968
Manufactured in the United States of America

---

1 2 3 4 5 6 7 8 9 10 KB 95 94 93 92 91 90 89 88 87 86

CONTENTS

FOREWORD

Dr. Werning is a man for whom Christianity is radical and exciting. As I read through the manuscript for this book, I experienced Werning at his best: the "can't sit still" Christian who is continually searching beyond the static values of his own culture to catch new and challenging glimpses of the radiant splendor of God at work in the world through His Word.

Introducing the concept of "supply-side stewardship," the author establishes God's supply house as the divine source of our entire being and every action. The "container model" of stewardship assumes that there is a fixed and limited supply to be divided, fought over, and redistributed. Werning explodes this culture-bound mentality with a Biblical revelation of God's unlimited and never-ending supply of both spiritual and material resources. His is the grace approach, vital to total Christian stewardship and to mission growth and outreach.

Werning calls for a dynamic plan of edifying and equipping. Education is the key. He calls for spiritual input that will produce stewardship output by God's grace output that glorifies God in service and giving. He deepens stewardship to a concept of unified and all-inclusive servanthood.

The author's stewardship is rooted in repentance, forgiveness, and renewal through a keen use of Law and Gospel. He brings Biblical theology and practice together. He exposes the negative and damaging nature of the maintenance mentality and model of church life, a model that stops short of a total acceptance of God's grace and detracts from and weakens the church in its outreach, its obedience to the Great Commission. He proposes a New Testament basis and grace principles for sanctification and stewardship activity.

Werning shows that the problem of the church is not a shortage of money, but a dearth of Biblical and spiritual knowledge and understanding of God's Word and will. He successfully challenges the institutional systems that have drained many a congregation of the vitality needed for aggressive world missions. He suggests a Biblical model for church renewal which adopts the priorities required for obedience to the Great Commission. He encourages the pursuit of excellence through the constant flow of God's grace. He goes far beyond traditional stewardship patterns as he combines proposals for education, prayer, discipline, and missions into an integrated process based on Biblical growth-presuppositions. He throws open the windows to give us a new view of the dynamics of creative spiritual leadership.

Fasten your seat belt and prepare yourself for a reading treat. Throw away your presuppositions and open yourself to the Spirit of God. Give yourself not only reading but also meditating time. Surely you will come out of this experience with a more complete and integrated model of both the theory and practice of receiving, living, and giving Christianity.

Eugene W. Bunkowske,
Ft. Wayne, Ind.

PREFACE

All of us have high ideals and great hopes for our congregation and the church generally. Don't all of us yearn for the simplicity of New Testament Christianity? We want the realization of obedience to the Great Commission of Jesus Christ. We desire to build congregations that are centers of world mission, experiencing dynamic worship, sacramental power, life-giving Bible study, enriching fellowship, commitment to ministry, and a life-style of evangelism and stewardship.

Mostly, it is a glorious vision unrealized. Do we need to be reminded that the vision has not been brought to reality? Within the first year of my graduation from seminary over 40 years ago my eyes were forcibly opened to the great chasm between the vision and reality, between purpose and practice.

There is no question about our sincerity, but religiosity had been substituted for spirituality more than we knew. There was an imbalance of form and living faith. It was time to ask whether we had an active, living, dynamic relationship with Christ through repentance and forgiveness or if we were living a religious routine and ritual. We seemed to be concerned with programs to the extent that we did not recognize that spiritual purpose and power were weakening.

We knew something was not right but did not know exactly what it was. We did not care to shatter our idealism by pursuing our questions too deeply, so ecclesiasticism or churchianity kept dissipating the spontaneity of our faith and vision. Through the years we have viewed the parade of nominal members and the deadwood for whom Law and Gospel have little meaning. Gradually we have seen some of the reasons for the impotence of the church to grapple with its mission to reach three billion people who do not confess Christ.

The vision is worthy and workable, for it comes from God. We can make better use of the Bible and get on with other pressing issues, developing healthy congregations committed to discipling their own members and all nations. It will be a struggle and will not come easy.

The maintenance activities of the organized church crowd out Biblical priorities and hamper total world mission outreach more than we know or care to admit. Charles E. Himmel tells about an acquaintance who said, "Your greatest danger is letting the urgent things crowd out the important." He calls it "the tyranny of the urgent.

Christianity suffers from such "tyranny of the urgent" whenever critical tasks for maintenance or survival demand immediate action. This deters us from the basic mission of the church: the essentials which feed and strengthen God's people to live like His people.

The dilemma goes much deeper than shortage of money. It is a problem of priorities. Congregations assume that since they are chartered as a Christian group they will naturally keep their true mission in perspective. But the sad fact is that "the tyranny of the urgent" causes many churches to major in minors and to use most of their energies on maintenance of the organization rather than on creative mission outreach.

Maintenance, demanding more money and more workers, pressures congregations into finding new and innovative methods rather than supplying them with a basic understanding of their mission. As a result, many congregations face three crises: (1) Meaning and purpose—what are our goals? (2) Beliefs—what is our Biblical basis for mission? (3) Authority—who is responsible for the fulfillment of the mission?

Organizational tendencies toward bureaucracy resist change. Everyone is inclined to the status quo. Most difficult is change in ourselves. If we can achieve that, we can change our church priorities, concepts, structures, and methods. Stewardship is the chief offender, as it centers mostly on finances because unpaid bills and unmet budgets seem the most urgent. The result is segmented and crippled church work.

Little wonder that for most people stewardship is a bad word.

The reason is that it is handled badly by many churches which have a maintenance mentality and an approach that depends on a "quick fix" to keep going another month, another year. This exhibits an addiction to stewardship mediocrity which suggests that we could settle our stewardship problems if only we had 13 months every year.

Failing to tackle the tough issues, and having jumbled priorities, there is an enslavement to a pietism which confuses the spiritual and the physical, the perceived and reality, the internal and external. This ignores the integrated and total life while it focuses on what the church needs to maintain its work at the present level or to progress minimally. Other people are deluded by statistics utilized in a way that soothes their consciences and satisfies their human expectations.

Many do not realize how trapped we are in the maintenance or survival model and how we have lost our ability and sensitivity for what is right and true in Biblical stewardship. We simply have not effectively identified the human and institutional control of the divine enterprise in many places.

Such an approach is a closed system with its own terminology. It fails to acknowledge that every idea has its consequences and that New Testament theology is revolutionary in its impact on Christian life and commitment. We build facades, emphasizing our stewardship achievements. But what about our servant accomplishments? What about the 50% to 70% who do not worship weekly in many congregations? Why is more attention given to the congregation's fiscal bankruptcy than to the spiritual bankruptcy of some of its members? Answer: The necessity to maintain the church and the attention given to the urgent.

One of the aberrations of our day is overdependence on material factors such as money and buildings. We are reminded of a cartoon that appeared in a British newspaper in the Great Depression of the 1930s, which referred to a situation in which economic stress and bank pressures caused such anxiety that people felt they were controlled by the banks. The cartoonist showed God, as he envisioned Him, with His arm around Jesus looking down at the people in their distress and saying, "My Son, we are defeated; the banks have spoken!" But the banks do not have the last word, neither do human factors of numbers and economic projections. Nor does money in the hands of a large number of people in a church guarantee success. The genuine success factor is divine power, the Holy Spirit working through the Word. This accounts for the eternal struggle between the traditional and Scriptural, between the structural and functional, between the institutional and divine factors.

This negative picture might suggest to the reader that this book is a protest. It is not. It is a proposal to church leaders everywhere to step back, take a long, honest look at what we are saying and doing in stewardship, challenge our assumptions, and recognize our misconceptions. No longer will we follow traditional patterns without question. Now we will reach for the highest ideals of God's Word.

Our proposal is to adopt a process and build a program which we call Supply-Side Stewardship, drawing from God's supply house with its limitless spiritual and material resources.

If that is done, the triviality and self-indulgence in the lives of many Christians will end. No longer will any church make God a technique for maintaining religious respectability instead of worshiping Him as the Source and Goal of our being. We will not wring our hands in despair or search for scapegoats.

Supply-Side Stewardship is written for all church leaders and active workers, to aid them toward creative leadership in congregations. At least 10% to 20% of the members of every church will benefit from reading and studying this message of God's great grace. Elders, deacons, stewardship, education, and evangelism leaders should review and consider these proposals concerning the life of grace which is free of human and institutional bondage.

The book is a companion to *Christian Stewards— Confronted and Committed* (Concordia Publishing House, 1982), which provides a Biblical theology and philosophical view of Christian stewardship. You may want to read it for a fuller picture of the grace approach to Christian stewardship.

Waldo J. Werning

CHAPTER ONE
FREE AND FIT FOR CHRIST'S MISSION

In order to fulfill the Great Commission, we are to be *one* that the world may be *won* (John 17:21). Such unity, gained by centering on God's Word and the Gospel of Jesus Christ, is our uniqueness. It is not an end in itself (maintenance), but necessary for world evangelization (mission outreach).

The basic task of the church is not only stewardship and service, but also worship, education, edification, and evangelism. The Great Commission of Jesus Christ is the unique purpose of the church and will unify the entire church program.

In order to have stewardship unified and integrated into the entire church program, it is imperative that there be a balance between (1) Bible teaching and worship, (2) fellowship and koinonia, and (3) evangelism and stewardship. Conversely, congregations are crippled by segmented, fractured, or unbalanced church emphases such as:

(1) When there is Bible teaching and worship alone: These churches are simply sterile Bible churches, which produce head knowledge that is reflected in dead orthodoxy, spiritual pride, and an argumentative spirit.

(2) Fellowship and koinonia areas alone: They emphasize relationships only, with little Biblical knowledge. This leads to a "rollercoaster" Christianity with emotional ups and downs and highs and lows.

(3) Evangelism and stewardship alone: Bible study and fellowship are neglected, starving people for the Word of God and Christian fellowship. As a result, the people do not grow spiritually. They easily feel pressured and burned out.

(4) Only (1) worship and Bible teaching and (2) fellowship and koinonia emphases: While neglecting Biblical stewardship and evangelism, people become ingrown and stagnant, accentuating the tendency toward spiritual pride and ignoring the afflictions of the world.

(5) Only (1) worship and Bible teaching and (3) evangelism and stewardship: Relationships and edifying are neglected, which results in soul-winners who relate mostly with the spiritual but not with people as human beings; their head knowledge does not lead to speaking the Word of Law and Gospel to each other in order to build the body of Christ.

(6) Only (2) fellowship and koinonia and (3) evangelism and stewardship emphases: These emphasize experiences and sharing, leaving Christians with no basis upon which to evaluate their "religious experiences," often leading to false doctrine. The "burn out" factor is very high as pep talks and back-slapping encouragements are too shallow to sustain any strength or momentum.

When all three of these segments are balanced to fulfill God's purpose for the church, they lead to a sound and effective ministry; church leaders will then demonstrate sound Biblical doctrine and content (preaching and practice), nurture (teaching, edifying), and fruits and gifts of the Spirit (priesthood of all believers, abilities, stewardship); they will be strong in evangelism and missions (reaching non-Christians according to Acts 1:8) and will use effective methods and efficient physical resources (good administration).

As theology is integrated with practice through the functional application of Biblical truth, the result will be strong stewardship action. Where there is segmentation and compartmentalization, there is little hope for sanctification with New Testament integrity.

If a congregation is to be strong in stewardship education and practice, there needs to be both a building of the spiritual life and a challenge for the expression of the Christian faith in the five essential tasks of the church: worship, teaching (nurture), edifying (fellowship), evangelizing, and service or stewardship.

Biblical Model for Church Renewal

Richard F. Lovelace provides a Biblical model for church renewal in his book, *Dynamics of Spiritual Life: An Evangelical Theology of Renewal:*

1. Three Conditions for Renewal:

(1) Awareness of the holiness of God: His justice and His love.

(2) Awareness of and repentance for sin: In your own life and in your community.

(3) Acceptance of full and free forgiveness in Christ.

2. Primary Elements of Renewal: In-Depth Presentation of the Gospel:

(1) Justification: You are accepted (in Christ).

(2) Sanctification: You are free from bondage to sin (in Christ). Faith will result in good works.

(3) The Indwelling Spirit: You are not alone (through Christ). God provides the strength.

(4) Authority in Spiritual Conflict: You have authority (in Christ).

3. Secondary Elements of Renewal: The Gospel at Work in the Church's Life:

(1) Mission: Following Christ into the world, presenting the Gospel in proclamation and in demonstration.

(2) Prayer: Expressing dependence on the power of His Spirit, individually and corporately.

(3) Community: Being in union with His Body in the congregation and in the church body.

(4) Disenculturation: Being free from cultural bonds (destructive and protective).

(5) Theological Calling: Having the mind of Christ (toward revealed truth and people).[1]

When the full dimensions of God's gracious provision in Christ are not clearly articulated, the church suffers distortion and weakness. When any essential dimension of what it means to be in Christ is obscured in the church's proclamation and life, there is little possibility that the members will understand or strive toward an experience of the fullness of the Christ-life.

Faith and Its Counterfeits

Donald G. Bloesch proposes that "true religion" or "true Christianity" anchored in the Gospel and the inerrant Word has counterfeits that propose alternatives or choices between what God and Satan want for us.[2] Since these counterfeits confuse and alienate those who desire Biblical stewardship, we need to understand how these counterfeits are harmful:

Legalism—A moral code and moralisms which destroy or pervert grace and freedom in Christ.

Formalism—Empty ritual that prevents true worship relating to the living Christ.

Humanitarianism—Mere service which draws attention away from spiritual care and Christian servanthood.

Enthusiasm—External signs that cover up the lack of internal reality.

Heroism—Supersaints that take away the significance of humble laborers.

We are concerned in this book about legalism, moralism, and perversion of grace especially with reference to their devastating effect on church stewardship practices. Without realizing it, the church has given the impression in stewardship that a dimension has been added for people to gain Christian fullness. Thus it may falsely appear that we are saved by grace through faith — plus stewardship works. Satan causes us to confuse sanctification as much as justification. The confusion of sanctification and stewardship practices needs careful attention by the church.

Reaching Beyond Behavior to Inner Reality

Far too many Christians and non-Christians perceive the Christian faith to be a behavior pattern instead of an inner regeneration which flows from inside to the outside. We focus on these two opposites:

Behavior	Behavior
Values	Values
Beliefs	Beliefs
	World View —

World View — What is real?	**Possessions** — use of things, car, boat, etc.
What is true (Gospel) What is good & best (Christ is first) What is done (Sanctification)	Trust God & man Material & rights have priority. Seek first own welfare & convenience
Regeneration — Inner Reality	**Spiritual Veneer —** Outward Behavior

Our world view, our attitude and way of looking at things, is reality to us. Whatever is in our inner being is what is most real to us. Christ is our Savior and our hope—our reality. Beliefs will reflect the Gospel and Biblical truths as our source and strength. Those beliefs will establish our values. Our values dictate our behavior. Behavior will be a reflection of the inner reality and the belief in Jesus.

Objectively observed, many Christians and churches in their programs misunderstand these factors about the nature of the Christian faith and life. They are sincere, yet their lives show that their Christianity is largely a spiritual veneer. Materialism, the things that can be touched, handled, bought, and sold, are what life is really all about, regardless of pious desires and platitudes. Cars, homes, paychecks, and boats are first concerns, while spiritual things are ceremonies and rituals. Indeed, Jesus Christ is often little more than a bubble in the outer circle of behavior—not the Center of a living relationship. He is merely the One we worship for an hour every one, two, or three weeks.

Churches in which such attitudes prevail look at the fruits as more important than the tree, at actions or deeds as more important than spiritual gifts. Stewardship is viewed in a legal framework, in which the responsibility of giving is stressed more than the inner condition of the soul. In such churches stewardship programs are vehicles for expanding all aspects of church work, rather than members' knowledge and faith. Superficially, they limit stewardship to what happens in the church building or in congregational programs. Moses, Gideon, Elijah, and Jeremiah could easily have hidden in these churches and escaped from their divinely assigned missions by their excuses which would readily be acceptable since mediocrity is so accepted: Moses, "I can't talk"; Gideon, "My family is the least of all, and I am the youngest"; Elijah, "There are so few of us and so many of them"; Jeremiah, "I'm too young."

Indeed, many churches are full of activities but empty of God's available supply: spiritual gifts, fruits of the Spirit, and discipling. Rather than words and deeds being a fervent confession of Christ, we find little denials of God's will day by day that are spiritually harmful.

Influence of Materialism

In his provocative book *The Golden Cow* John White makes shocking conclusions about the materialism of the 20th-century church: "The stern denunciations of the prophets and the violent action of Jesus in the Temple stir us only in the way pictures in an art gallery do. We view them with wondering eyes, marveling that such dramatic power, such beauty can exist; yet as we pass into the hubbub of the streets, we leave the pictures behind."[3] How would we respond if one of the Bible's prophets jumped from those pages to confront today's churches and their members? At what point should the Son of God become enraged? If Isaiah, Jeremiah, Ezekiel, and Hosea accused Israel of apostasy and spiritual prostitution with the world, we should not be surprised that our generation is immersed with materialism which needs to be exposed by God's Word. Certainly, God's justice and love face Christians and the church when guilty of holding material things in higher regard than Him, when our priorities often favor the material rather than the spiritual. Recall that Jesus Himself fearlessly defied the established religious system and authority where it had strayed from the truth.

As the system flourished under the temple hierarchy in Jesus' day, so stewardship methods are generally utilized as a system today. Author White challenges the materialism, institutionalism, ceremonialism, and organizational dependence of our times by referring to the "uncanny similarity between our day and that of ancient Israel."

White continues:

> God's ancient people worshipped the Baalim: we worship a materialistic golden cow. At heart many of us have a greed for things. We have made the world's agenda of status-seeking our own. Unquestioningly, we have adapted the world's techniques of gaining influence and security. And it has worked. We are flushed with success. . . . Another Temple cleansing is needed.
>
> Jesus warned His followers about forgetting to whom they belong and of selling themselves to mammon. Against commercialized desecration of the Temple He acted violently, expressing the same moral reprehension that inspired earlier prophets to call God's people a whore.
>
> The Twentieth-Century Church has also forgotten which master she belongs to, painting herself like a hussy in her silly pursuit of Lord Mammon. Or, to use another image, the church has gone a-whoring after a golden cow.
>
> Not a calf, if you please, but a cow. I call her a *golden* cow because her udders are engorged with liquid gold, especially in the West where she grazes in meadows lush with greenbacks. Her priests placate her by slaughtering godly principles upon whose blood she looks with tranquil satisfaction. Anxious rows of worshippers bow down before their buckets. Although the gold squirts endlessly, the worshippers are trembling lest the supply of sacrificial victims should one day fail to appease her.
>
> When I talk about worshipping the golden cow, I am talking about a particular form of materialism to which we have fallen prey. It is a way of life that sets our feet on the road to spiritual harlotry.
>
> Our days are spent earning money to pay for the cars we bought, and the evenings and weekends to spending more money, the money we hope to earn tomorrow. Our grasping arms are being crammed with the produce of an age of abundance, our eagerness to grasp being more than matched by the zeal of the people who would shower such produce upon us. Abundance in the West has become a menace threatening to inundate us under tons of television sets, houses, clothes, flowery toilet paper, cars, snowmobiles, books, furniture.
>
> There is nothing wrong, of course, with a proper distribution of goods and services. I am not talking about that but about the promotion of superabundance. . . . We are no longer His creatures accepting and distributing the goodness He pours upon us but the feverish and slavish worshippers of abundance itself.
>
> The god of greed is a cheat. His promise of material rewards may never even be kept. He cheats his priests as much as he cheats his worshippers, turning his back on both and leaving them to their despair once he no longer has use for them. And even those upon

> whom he lavishes his rewards find them strangely flat. His flowers are made of plastic and his food of sawdust, while his wine can neither be fresh nor intoxicate. His delights have the power to dazzle and excite but they can satisfy nobody.
>
> What does it all boil down to? It comes to this: we Christians are too often like sponges soaked to capacity with the value system of the society we live in. . . . The greatest good in life is a bigger (or better-cooked) slice of this world's pie, a pie to which we all have an inalienable right. And it is precisely here, in our unconscious acceptance of a false value system (with its confusion about our "rights") that the root of the problem lies.
>
> Let the preachers remind the church again that no one can serve two masters! Never mind the congregation members who get sore and defensive.
>
> If our harlotry were private, if we were to worship the gods of materialism in the secrecy of our hearts or even of our household, the matter would be bad enough. But it is inevitable that, blinded as we are to our error, we have molded our churches by the values that govern our own lives.
>
> Because Christian organizations are property centered, their program becomes property bound. Once you have bought an expensive building, you have to justify its existence. . . . They are (without realizing it) our masters rather than our servants. They sit on our boards and committees and cast their silent votes on every motion. . . . Money from people all around them pours into Operation Big Deal.
>
> It is not possessing riches that God condemns, but clinging to them, coveting them and having our activity centered around them. It is our wrong way of looking at things, our wrong scale of values, that matters. It is not meeting in a building that is wrong, but making such a building a priority and fooling ourselves into believing that we can't get on without it . . . . Churches should rethink priorities.

Author White admits that he may seem to be generalizing and oversimplifying very complex matters, but there is much substance in his observations. He writes: "We are thinking as the world thinks. We see money as more important than it really is. Money is powerless to generate spiritual activity, and lack of money powerless to cramp it. We have forgotten to listen to God's plans and totally underestimated His power."[4]

We should not be surprised that we often feel half empty and uneasy about our church accomplishments, for Christians are rarely happy as materialists. The New Man wants to be unshackled, and the divine tugs at us vigorously. We find ourselves apologizing for larger homes, new cars, and the abundance we are seeking. It makes us ill at ease, and it lies at the root of our ineffectiveness.

Few of us are willing to open our eyes fully to the ugly war within us. Our old nature helps us to pretend it does not exist. We live with two irreconcilable world views at the center: the greatness of God and the fascination of everyday life. So we share radiant smiles and give warm Christian handshakes, not really understanding that God can easily supply all our needs, if we walk the faith road. We devote energies mainly to advancing church causes and institutional needs, however dubious they may be. The weapons of our warfare are promotional materials, campaigns and drives.

The prophet Hosea reminded God's people in the Old Testament "They made idols for their own destruction" (8:4 RSV). So we have idols which many do not recognize and will not admit. In some cases we have chosen substitutes—the created—for the Creator. We have turned to *things* more than we care to admit. We have established a hierarchy of values directed by the outer circle of behavior influenced by the world's ethics more than by the inner circle of our Christian faith. Our unfortunate idolatries have helped form the framework of our understanding and action in church practice.

Challenge All Assumptions

There is a need to challenge all assumptions and preconceptions. Much tradition, both good and bad, has developed in the stewardship program of churches. It is time to evaluate our stewardship messages and methods so that we might reach for the highest ideals of God's Word. Traditional patterns that have been adopted without little question or by rationalizations and negative thinking must be scrutinized.

There is a need to be open and totally honest in our appraisal of the institutional situation. Our observations have been tested by years of close contact with pastors and with congregations and their leaders. Indeed, some of our statistics and many observations have been suggested by thousands of participants in groups to whom we have spoken or for whom we have been consultant.

Purified by the Gospel

Stewardship can be kept from degeneration only by an insistence that it penetrate the heart and be based on the Word, transforming all of life by contact at the root. Defective stewardship theology may galvanize the emotions to move people's wills toward obedience, but this leads to manipulation through hard-sell salesmanship and the rest of the trappings of stewardship methodology. It is tainted by the sinful cultural diseases of covetousness, gluttony, pride, and greed so characteristic of our day. Only as the spotlight of God's Word is turned on the individual fleshly manifestations of disobedience will there be any hope for repentance among Christians, who should be leading stewardship transformation, affecting also the entire earth. The fleshly patterns, which in some places have been accepted as normal modes of behavior, have blocked spiritual energy and have blinded us to false stewardship values. Counterfeit faith and counterfeit stewardship must be recognized and exposed as a perversion of grace.

Only by the Gospel of grace can stewardship be purified and brought into the service of the kingdom of Christ. The Gospel blocks all self-devised efforts to gain holiness. It proclaims through Word and sacrament a free promise of grace made available by an act of God in the atonement of Jesus, after which follows a life of sanctification. The new birth gives a quickening "Yes!" to the things of God and the hardest "No!" to the pride of man.

Adolph Koeberle says: "We can neither create nor maintain the new life, but we can always lose it. The whole idea of becoming good through doing good is excluded."[5]

When justification by faith is not adequately understood, the result is an insecurity that creates sufficient pious forms and actions to pacify the conscience and to quiet the sense of alienation from God. Romans 6 makes clear that the basis of sanctification is our union with Christ in His death and resurrection, in which the old nature is put down and a new nature is created for newness of life. Without a secure faith in Christ, people will fulfill their "church obligation" by sitting in pews and listening passively. They may use the catchwords of the church, but have too little awareness of what it is all about. Their false understanding of the Christian life, focusing on behavior and externals, will respond with a frantic clinging to past traditions when confronted with change. Theirs is a desperate effort to maintain allegiance to church rules or to methods. Christianity is then a behavior pattern more than an inner reality based on regeneration of life through Christ.

Unless we stop leaning on legalistic and moralistic stewardship and begin to lean fully on Jesus Christ in a servant life-style, our spiritual lives and the mission of the church will continue to be short-circuited. Legalism goes arm in arm with a type of sanctification that has jumped the grace track to its own track of mixed works and grace.

Our goal is to see members growing in sanctification and making progress at conquering sin in their lives. This growth in grace and faith must look to Christ for overcoming personal problems and for fulfilling the real purpose of our lives. Moralism fails in this endeavor, for whether it takes the form of denunciation or pep talks, it ultimately can create only awareness of sin and guilt or at best manufacture virtues built on will power.

Biblical sanctification (living for Christ) becomes part of the Good News, the victory over the flesh won by faith in Christ, and it relies on His Spirit for power over sin. Stewardship which attacks only the surface of sin and fails to establish spiritual growth in the believer's union with Christ produces either self-righteousness or despair. Both of these conditions poison or weaken the spiritual life.

In the next chapter we will consider the dilemma we face: We live in time and are subject to change, but God inhabits eternity and is unchangeable. We are sinful and weak, but He is holy and strong. We tread on holy ground and must remove our sandals, walking softly with heads bowed low, ready to fall on our knees if need be. His justice burns against those who hold material things in higher regard than the spiritual. He is also full of mercy and love in forgiving us. We must remember from where we have come and to whom we belong. The Holy Spirit Himself will reveal to us what we are to do.

CHAPTER TWO

TWO OPTIONS: MAINTENANCE OR SUPPLY-SIDE

Two choices face us for our motivations, objectives, goals, methods, and strategies in our church work and in our personal lives: a maintenance-survival approach or a supply-side approach, the traditional or the Scriptural.

The maintenance model is anxious about budgets, needs, and institutional goals, while faith is often transformed into duty and oppressive obligations. As one layman told us, this makes the church a pressure cooker with psychological and emotional mechanisms to integrate members into the system more than into the body of Christ. Thus we depend more on man's supply house than on God's supply house, making stewardship more a matter between man and the institution than between man and God.

Our proposal is to destroy the maintenance mentality and model. In its place we build a program called Supply-Side Stewardship. Then the Word is the central force of stewardship. That Word offers God's supply of love and mercy, which is unbelievable and fantastic! He supplies power for victory over sin, the devil, and the world. The greatness and goodness of the Triune God is not always properly understood, so we often fail to tap the necessary supply to perform the stewardship and mission tasks assigned to us. This happens because of overdependence on human strength and resources while God's generous bounty is not fully utilized. The result is that there are few true servants, in the Scriptural sense, and that the church lacks a support system for all those in need of special help. In the meantime such churches are struggling with their pygmy budgets and are facing endless deficits.

God's Supply House

Paul prays that the Ephesians (1:17–23) may know their unlimited resources, for they cannot tap resources of which they are unaware: " . . . what are the riches of the glory of His inheritance in the saints, and what is the exceeding greatness of His power toward us who believe, according to the working of His mighty power which He worked in Christ . . . . And He put all things under His feet. . . ." Paul writes in Eph. 3:14–21 about our possession of inner strength, the indwelling Christ, incomprehensible love, infinite fullness and internal power: " . . . to be strengthened with might through His Spirit in the inner man, that Christ may dwell in your hearts through faith; that you . . . may be able to comprehend with all the saints what is the width and length and depth and height — to know the love of Christ which passes knowledge; that you may be filled with all the fullness of God. Now to Him who is able to do exceedingly abundantly above all that we ask or think, according to the power that works in us, to Him be glory in the church by Christ Jesus throughout all ages, world without end." Little wonder that, after Paul has shown the divine resources, he tells us our function as he exhorts: "I, therefore, the prisoner of the Lord, beseech you to walk worthy of the calling with which you were called . . . . But to each of us grace was given according to the measure of Christ's gift" (Eph. 4:1, 7).

Looking at this divine Source, we believe that God has supplied His people with all the spiritual and material resources required to get the saving Gospel of Jesus Christ to all people in the world in our lifetime. With God as our Source we shall never lack the spiritual or material resources to reach the unregenerate multitudes in all the earth (locally and worldwide) in our generation. J. Hudson Taylor knew that when churches or missions lack sufficient supply to reach non-Christians effectively, they have failed to avail themselves of God's supply. He said: "God's work done in God's way will never lack God's supply."

God told Abraham of this rich supply and its function in the world: "I will bless you . . . and you shall be a blessing . . . . And in you all the families of the earth shall be blessed" (Gen. 12:2–3). As children of Abraham who put their faith in Jesus, we are blessed with believing Abraham: "In you all the nations shall be blessed" (Gal. 3:8). It can be stated another way: "I will supply you, and you will be a supplier to many."

In view of God's great resources, how is it possible that we as a Christian minority in the world enjoy and retain in our own reservoir the constant flow of God's grace, love, and mercy in Jesus Christ for the forgiveness of our sins while the unbelieving majority do not enjoy the spiritual wealth which God wants to share with them through us? We simply have not adequately understood the Great Commission of our Lord Jesus Christ. Dr. Donald McGavran, the father and founder of the Church Growth Movement, is right when he makes the shocking statement: "There is general disobedience of the Great Commission of our Lord Jesus Christ in Christendom today."

What other supply house can use so many superlatives and offer so much? "God is able to make all grace abound toward you, that you, always having all sufficiency in all things, have an abundance for every good work" (2 Cor. 9:8). There is no way that a Christian can call himself poor and weak. Paul reminds us: "Now may He who supplies seed to the sower, and bread for food, supply and multiply the seed you have sown and increase the fruits of your righteousness, while you are enriched in everything for all liberality, which causes thanksgiving through us to God. For the administration of this service not only supplies the needs of the saints, but also is abounding through many thanksgivings to God, while, through the proof of this ministry, they glorify God for the obedience of your confession to the gospel of Christ, and for your liberal sharing with them and all men . . ." (2 Cor. 9:10–13). This clearly shows God's marvelous plan, through which He enriches us and others.

God could have used angels to do the job, for He has armies of them. He could have tuned us to His Word individually or in groups as He wills, but He chose not to do so. He decided to give us great worth not only in redemption but in our service to others by His grace and power. Thus it glorifies Him when others offer thanksgiving to God for our love in action. Here we see the functional nature of God's supply program.

We can learn of the "all-ness" of God's part in our success: "So then neither he who plants is anything, nor he who waters, but God who gives the increase" (1 Cor. 3:7). Paul writes in 1 Cor. 4:7: "For who makes you differ from another? And what do you have that you did not receive? Now if you did indeed receive it, why do you glory as if you had not received it?"

As for those who say that "the church is always asking for money," Paul reminds them that the need is theirs to give, not God's to get: "God, who made the world and everything in it, since He is Lord of heaven and earth, does not dwell in temples made with hands. Nor is He worshiped with men's hands, as though He needed anything, since He gives to all life, breath, and all things" (Acts 17:24–25).

That God can and will provide all our spiritual and material needs from His storehouse is the assurance of this amazing promise: "My God shall supply all your need according to His riches in glory by Christ Jesus" (Phil. 4:19). This is the incredible resource which offers us the Bank of Heaven itself, where we cannot overdraw our account, we cannot write a check too big, and we cannot break the bank. God offers us blank checks signed in the blood of Jesus Christ, who invites us: "Ask, and it will be given to you . . . . For everyone who asks receives . . ." (Matt. 7:7–8). " . . . how much more will your Father who is in heaven give good things to those who ask Him!" (v. 11). Not wanting us to limit our lives and His work by tapping only limited human resources, He insists: "If you abide in Me, and My words abide in you, you will ask what you desire, and it shall be done for you. By this My Father is glorified, that you bear much fruit" (John 15:7–8).

David's great doxology in 1 Chron. 29 (vv. 10–19) exalts God as the true and complete Resource for everything that we do here on earth. David had given great gifts with all his might. His love was for the house of the Lord, giving over and above all that he had prepared for that holy house. The people offered generously because of their loyal hearts. Then we hear David praising God, worshiping Him for His greatness, power, glory, and majesty. He says: “All that is in heaven and in earth is Yours. . . . Both riches and honor come from You, and You reign over all. In Your hand is power and might; in Your hand it is to make great and to give strength to all.” David continues with an attitude that suggests that He thinks, *What’s the big deal, God, that we have brought all of this to You? Why should we receive any credit at all?* He writes: “But who am I, and who are my people, that we should be able to offer so willingly as this? For all things come from You, and of Your own we have given. You. . . . All this abundance that we have prepared to build You a house for Your holy name is from Your hand, and is all Your own.”

Yet many gripe and groan about serving and giving to God. They need to hear from the Supply House Keeper: “Every beast of the forest is Mine, and the cattle on a thousand hills. . . . If I were hungry, I would not tell you; for the world is Mine, and all its fullness. . . . Offer to God thanksgiving, and pay your vows to the Most High. Call upon Me in the day of trouble; I will deliver you, and you shall glorify Me” (Ps. 50:10–15). Of course, God would not ask us for food if He were hungry. It’s His supply house.

God has made a covenant with us in Christ to supply us with every spiritual and material need for our daily lives and for His church. How often does He have to repeat it before we will believe? “Oh, the depth of the riches both of the wisdom and knowledge of God! How unsearchable are His judgments and His ways past finding out! For who has known the mind of the Lord? Or who has become His counselor? Or who has first given to Him and it shall be repaid to him? For of Him and through Him and to Him are all things, to whom be glory forever. Amen” (Rom. 11:33–36).

As God gives the supply or gifts, use them. He tells us: “As each one has received a gift, minister it to one another, as good stewards of the manifold grace of God. If anyone speaks, let him speak as the oracles of God. If anyone ministers, let him do it as with the ability which God supplies, that in all things God may be glorified through Jesus Christ, to whom belong the glory and the dominion forever and ever. Amen” (1 Peter 4:10–11). As Christians find their resources and supply, they will know their task, their purpose, their destiny in life. The total of all members’ supply of abilities and money will direct the church to its potential ministry and mission.

We need to stop appealing to members for support of partial

and limited ministries, which expect low response from the maintenance mentality of half-defeated, half-victorious Christians. As the individual abilities and gifts and the corporate gifts of all the members come from God's supply house, they help create new ministries and mission avenues. God is able to do far more than we ever ask or think.

Intake and Output

God intends for us to be channels for the flow of His grace and mercy, providers of spiritual and material blessings to all those in need in the world. "His compassions fail not. They are new every morning; great is Your faithfulness" (Lam. 3:22–23).

Contradicting and off-setting God's plan for full supply in our own lives and the work of His church is the maintenance model and traditional stewardship forms, "having a form of godliness but denying its power" (2 Tim. 3:5). This usually finds 80% of the members to be underachievers in relation to their God-given abilities, possibly 90% weak in witnessing, and 99% not active in planned evangelism, with 97-1/2% of their incomes kept for themselves. That's why the body of Christ in its organizational form of the church is often ineffective and inefficient.

God's plan is that we "may grow up in all things into Him who is the head — Christ — from whom the whole body, joined and knit together by what every joint supplies, according to the effective working by which every part does its share, causes growth of the body for the edifying of itself in love" (Eph. 4:15–16). Notice here that God has planned that every member or part of His body supplies something important for the whole. The fact is that 70% to 80% of the members of most churches are incapable of edifying and are poor suppliers to others.

Fortunately, the positive side reveals the strong faith and great dedication of that minority of believers in each congregation who reveal spiritual maturity as leaders. Some set a wonderful example of humble service, faithful witnessing, and generous giving. The unfortunate thing is that the faithful ones are such a small percentage of the total membership.

We look now at the difference between the traditional and the Scriptural, between the maintenance and supply-side stewardship models.

The Two Stewardship Models

Basic Contrasts

TRADITIONAL STEWARDSHIP (Maintenance)	SCRIPTURAL STEWARDSHIP (Supply-Side)
Method-Message-Theology	Theology-Message-Method

In my first pastorate we started with needs and a budget, after which I preached a message on Christian giving tied to those needs. Then we made special appeals to make that budget. Later I learned that we should first start with Biblical theology, and develop a Law-Gospel message with Biblical principles. After that we are to find a method that will allow us to reach every member with that message.

GIVING TO (Needs, Budgets, Church)	GIVING FROM (What God Gives), Then Through the Church

The "to" approach is the essence of the traditional model, in which we entreat and cajole people to give to this and to that need in the church, and meeting budgets becomes the criterion for all members — faithful or otherwise. The "from" approach has the Biblical emphasis on identifying each individual's gifts and then using these gifts through the church or other mission agencies.

Man's View (External)	God's View (Internal)

Man is such an earthbound creature, often depending more on human eyes than on spiritual sight, who like an earthworm or snail crosses roads and sidewalks which are filled with danger, instead of staying in the safe areas. The New Man depends upon the vertical dimension, God's Word, with spiritual insights directed by the Holy Spirit. He can see above the human horizontal plane, having his eyes sharpened and his mind enlightened to discern things from a spiritual perspective.

Keep from Losing (Hold the Territory)	Send Out to Gain (Gain New Territory)

Wanting to secure the turf we have won by our own efforts and management, we finish with a holding operation instead of going faithfully with Father Abraham to more lands, as God has promised.

Tap and Sap Human Resources	Tap Divine Resources Without Sapping Human Resources

Human efforts by leaders and active members have caused endless stress. Fully tapping God's supply house assures that human resources will not be sapped.

Motivation

Appeal for Loyalty to Missions	God's Love in Christ Is the Cause of Stewardship Action

There are many good reasons to give, but there is only one basic Christian motivation, namely, God's love for us in Christ Jesus in the forgiveness of our sins. His love triggers and empowers our love to go into action.

Legalistic Measures Which Commingle Law and Gospel, Moralizing, Demanding	Balanced Use of Law and Gospel

This is the real test of leadership — the proper dividing of Law and Gospel, with distinctions made in their use.

Rules and Regulations, or Commands for Each to Do His Part	Covenant, Promise, Old Man-New Man, Repentance-Forgiveness

The key to strong stewardship is sharing the gracious

promises of God with God's covenant people, showing the victory of the New Man over the Old Man by the Spirit's work, encouraging daily repentance and renewal through forgiveness.

Prosperity Creates Better Stewardship	Faith Will Determine What Percentage of Income We Give to God

Better incomes never have and never will produce better givers. Faith determines what we will give: The stronger the faith, the higher the percentage; the weaker the faith, the lower the percentage. Our prayer is, "Lord, increase my faith," not, "Lord, increase my income so I can give more."

Objectives and Goals

Raise Money	Raise Men

Money-raising campaigns and drives are not the solution to the church's financial needs. Raise people spiritually, and you will raise money too. Giving is a byproduct of spiritual growth.

Extend Our Own Little Local Kingdom by Providing for Our Little Projects or Self-Interest in God's Work	Extend the Kingdom of Christ Locally and Worldwide Through God's Supply House, by the Gospel
Focus on What the *Church* Wants	Focus on what *God* Wants

The result is that the church gets what it wants, but God doesn't get what He wants.

Get the Church Job Done	Individual Spiritual Growth (Edify Fellow Members)

There is a world of difference between merely getting

the church job done (as perceived by people who use Bible texts for inspiration to help them achieve minimum goals) and enlisting every individual member in Bible study for spiritual growth to make them capable of edifying one another.

Better Church Members — Stronger Christians

We inappropriately talk about good and bad church members, and try to make better church members. The Biblical objective is to make stronger Christians, growing in grace and faith and knowledge of the Lord Jesus Christ.

Allow Christians to Bring Excuses — Teach Christians How to Bear Fruit

According to the practice of many members at present, Judgment Day will find people standing before the throne of God making all types of excuses for not serving or giving more because of their human circumstances — excuses which God finds unacceptable, although they were accepted in congregations. Jesus will remind these people: "You did not choose Me, but I chose you and appointed you that you should go and bear fruit . . . that . . . should remain" (John 15:16).

Struggling with Leftovers — Fruits of Production

Maintenance is the enemy of full productivity. Maintenance finds every cause fighting for its share of gifts, which average possibly about 2-1/2% of personal income. Jesus' parables tells of productivity which offers sufficient resources for fulfilling mission tasks. Believers are called and empowered for full productivity (Eph. 2:10).

Use Budgets to Get Gifts — Pre-Budget Program

One of the misuses of budgets is to place the budget

"thermometer" on the church walls and halls or with the financial records published in the weekly bulletin. What impression is the worshiper to gain from such prominence of dollar needs and expectations? Obviously, that money is the big concern and priority of the congregation.

Budgets are spending guides, not collection guides. Therefore the educational program in Christian giving should precede setting the budget or informing the people what the budget may be. The people actually set the budget by their commitment in planned, first-fruit, proportionate giving.

Small Parts of Life and Resources	Entire Life

We sometimes get so excited when one person or another gives just a little part of his or her life, as though we can keep portions for selfish purposes. All of our lives are to be lived to the glory of God in physical, social, material, abilities, and relational areas.

Acquire a Few More Dollars to Meet Increased Budget Needs	Change Giving Habits

When making a budget, we may fail to note that possibly 60% to 70% of the people in the congregation may have been robbing God while a small minority have been giving generous firstfruit gifts. The focus needs to be on the individuals who need to change giving habits.

Your Share of the Budget	God's Share of Your Income

Maintenance-minded people always talk about the need to do one's share in reaching the budget, but God's Word encourages us to give God His share of our income, regardless of what that might be.

Group Financial Results (Producers)	Individual Fruit (Fruit Bearers)

Maintenance leaders treat members as producers rather than the fruit bearers of which Jesus speaks in John 15.

Gain Service for Church Activities	Make Disciples for Sharing Christ Every Moment of Life

Concepts (Content and Message)

Present Church as a Good Institution That Needs to Be Supported	The Church as the Body of Christ

Our institutionalized form of stewardship has actually beclouded and confused the nature and function of the body of Christ. Few people really understand 1 Cor. 12, Romans 12, and Eph. 4.

Plead for People to *Support* Christianity	True Nature of Christianity: We *are* Christians

The word "support" has been tied to institutional claims and actually confuses what the church and Christianity are all about. We are not called to support Bible study programs, witnessing programs, and stewardship programs, which are all true functions of being a Christian. We *are* Christians, not members who support Christianity. How ridiculous to invite people to support our Bible class program. The homemaker does not invite the family to a meal by saying, "Come, support my cooking program," but rather, "Come, eat!" God's invitation is, "Come, eat the Word!"

Stress the Ability and Potential of People to Serve or to Give by Enlarging Their Loyalty to God	Ability of God to Serve or Give Through People

Loyalty banquets should not challenge the loyalty of people, but should find us challenging and accepting the loyalty and promises of God. The question is whether we believe that God is faithful to His promises. A Christian answers, "I believe God is faithful and able to do this work through me."

Terminology

A University of Nebraska sociology professor, speaking to a church's couple's club, stated: "You can tell a person's concepts and understanding by the terminology he uses." The same is true of Christian stewardship.

Fair Shares, Needs, Dues Quotas, Contributions	Offerings, Proportionate Giving, First Fruits, Tithing, Worshipful Giving

The maintenance side deals with institutional loyalty, while the supply side concerns itself with faithfulness to Biblical principles.

Pledges, Financial Drives and Campaigns	Faith Promise, Commitment, "New Steps of Faith," Educational Program

Campaigns and drives are so closely identified with institutional goals that we need to seek Biblical terms which reflect Biblical concepts as we speak.

Encouragement to "Go Over the Top"	Encouragement to Exceed the "Minimum Goal" or the Work Program

Our dwarf budgets have never been the "top," so why do we encourage people to help us "go over the top"? Such budgets have been bare minimum, bare bottom, so we need to be honest and avoid statements which confuse the entire issue.

Methods

Ask for Volunteers to Serve	Challenge All to Discover and Use Their Spiritual Gifts

The call for volunteers has found the church with 70% to 80% underachievers and the need to pressure people to respond. As we change the focus, allowing individuals to discover their God-given gifts, members will feel the need to study God's Word more faithfully, seek to understand their relationship with God, and strive to have a growing faith.

Make Stewardship a One-Time Promotional Effort	Stewardship Training Is a Part of Christian Growth and Sanctification

An annual promotional effort has never been adequate. We need to understand stewardship as a part of sanctification (Christian living).

Campaigns and Programs for Money	An Educational Process by Which All Members Are Learning the Grace of Giving
Legalistic, Man-Imposed Devices That Seek to Declare One's Share for the Church	Let the Holy Spirit Guide and Empower Through Clear Teaching of the Word

There are real dangers in establishing quotas and suggested goals, because they rely too much upon the judgment of men rather than the power of God. We should never tell people, "The committee is asking you to think in terms of giving $——." Having a concern for the spiritual attitude and understanding of the giver, we share God's principles and encourage him to consider God's will faithfully.

Money for the Church	People for God
Success Gimmicks	Biblical Principles

Our files are filled with human plans to gain more money and with gimmicks that are called successful because they seem to produce more money. However, God's Word must dictate our stewardship message and method, which is all we need.

Sales and Bazaars	All Resources of All Members According to Christian Stewardship Concepts

Sales and bazaars are ingrained in the life of the church, and many are faithfully giving of their time to these efforts. These same consecrated efforts, time and service, can be donated in other ways so that all of the resources of all our members will be utilized for God's service.

Give God the	Place God *First*

Leftover giving is the trademark of maintenance stewardship. Giving to God first is the only principle which has God's blessing.

Pledge of a Certain *Amount*	Commit a Certain *Percentage* to God

Amounts do not mean a thing unless you understand *from* what they were given. Both the Old and the New Testaments deal with portions or percentages.

Consider Giving a *Burden*	Christian Giving Is a Joy, an *Expression of Faith*

Stewardship acts are sometimes treated as necessary burdens we must undertake for God. If someone would consider work as a necessary burden and then was relegated for the rest of life to a rocking chair, the rocking chair would be the real burden. The joy is to get out of the spiritual rocking chair and to exercise and express our Christian faith.

Needs in Search of Givers	Givers in Search of Needs

Acts 4:33 – 35 reminds us that great grace and great power produced great witness. It then reveals that this same immense grace changed the Christians into givers who were in search of needs.

Battle of the Budgets and Financial Pies	Teach Personal Money Management and Personal Financial Planning

The maintenance model finds many churches, organizations, and groups fighting for the same dollars. Budgets are carefully calculated, some portions are cut short, and each cause gets less of the financial pie. Instead, all Christians need to be taught proper handling of their total income so that every portion is enlarged and used to the glory of God.

Fruit Pickers	Caretakers Who Dig and Fertilize

We have tended to be fruit pickers, sometimes even pounding the tree to glean more fruit to feed the family of God. Christ's parable tells us that our responsibility is to dig and fertilize. He told of the owner who saw that a tree was not bearing fruit. The owner called the caretaker, asking, "Why does this tree not bear fruit? Cut it down and let it make room for a fruit-bearing tree." The caretaker pleaded, "Give it a season, a year, and let me dig and fertilize." Leaders are the caretakers who need to plead to God for time to plan their educational process and program—the digging and fertilizing approach.

Scope of the Work (Object of Giving)

Either . . . or	Both . . . and (Acts 1:8)

Many members will plead, "Either we do our local work effectively and then the world mission will have to suffer, or we do more for world missions and the local work will be hampered." Not so Jesus, who said that we are to be witnesses *both* in Jerusalem (locally) *and* in Judea (in the state or province in which we live) *and* in Samaria (the other states and provinces of our country) *and* to the ends of the earth. In order to be faithful to this commission, He has also given the provision in Acts 1:8: "You shall receive power when the Holy Spirit has come upon you."

Nibblers of the Possible	Grabbers of the Impossible

The maintenance approach finds us setting attainable goals in service and giving, working with pygmy budgets related to world mission needs, while in our church council and voters' meetings we argue and debate whether even this is possible. Supply-side mentality looks at the limitless resources and energy from God, who desires to do what is impossible from our viewpoint. One finds us dealing with man's word while the other deals with God's Word.

The maintenance approach has caused us to do stewardship patchwork, patching one program during one crisis and another program during another crisis, and sometimes even patching the patches. Supply-side makes a new garment, a creative educational approach, which builds and trains the saints according to Eph. 4. God's constant flow of love through the Body in action is the Biblical model for us to consider.

Summary of the Two Approaches

Approach One

Approach One stresses results and group performance with $$ as the product. Spiritual growth is only a by-product. Subtle and not-so-subtle legalisms abound. Sanctification is confused.

The maintenance approach produces ambiguity in matters of grace, opens temptations to continued idolatries, offers human constructs, ideas, and ideals, and allows religious egocentric strivings to replace Biblical truths. It is an anthropocentric kind of spirituality. There is more emphasis on man's ascent to God than God's descent to man.

The tendency is to lose our first love by keeping eyes on worldly factors more than on God. Spiritual and earthly kingdoms are subtly fused together in a gradual process of compromise, allowing the spiritual to be infected by culture. Members easily become crippled by fear and doubt about the human capacity to do the job. There is empty formalism or barren Biblicism that quickly degenerates into oppressive legalism.

Here we find perfectionist enthusiasm or frenetic activism that borders on humanism. It drives to discontentment and halfway measures, that is, "I'll give *some* time, abilities, money, self." But there is no "death to self," but rather a struggle to survive.

There is encouragement of the pursuit of pleasure (concentrating on external things, material, personal gain, regardless of consequence) more than an emphasis on holiness or real happiness (inner peace and joy, flow of grace, being possessed fully by Christ).

People easily become embroiled in behavior concerns and personalities that center on codes and on "fairness" rather than on the substance of faith. Faith is then transformed into duty; we seek to keep the Gospel treasure and the Great Commission obligation safe in a subtle cage of rules.

These legalistic maintenance attitudes and approaches are cloaked in many guises: misguided dogmatism, false asceticism (individual piety and works conceived as meritorious in God's sight), vigorism (church activities made into standards and inflexible expectations or even substituted for the third use of the Law). There is a concentration on duty (Luke 17:9 – 10) without balance between Biblical norms and the Holy Spirit's power.

Formalism, which also thrives under the maintenance model, accepts and speaks the doctrine without true evangelical practice. There is more interest in "ritual sacrifice" and "burnt offerings" than the sacrifices of a broken and contrite heart and being right with one's fellow man (Ps. 51:15 – 19; Matt. 5:23 – 24). It allows for formalistic preaching, praying, and counseling that easily becomes dead orthodoxy.

The maintenance approach also encourages false securities and hopes: Comfort is taken in gaining achievements, recognition, positions, titles, superior knowledge, more material possessions, storehouses of food and clothing, association or identification with a select group of people. These actually result in insecurity, hopeless attitudes, man-pleasing, hypocrisy, defensiveness, and comparison with others.

The maintenance approach or model inordinately attaches stewardship to the human supply, pressuring people with institutional promotion and propaganda. The church has institutionalized stewardship by methods and management on the basis of man's supply rather than God's. The commitment to the church as an organization has produced the herd instinct, as people's loyalty is judged on the basis of how closely they follow the church herd. There is a greater concern to help the church than to help people.

Approach One is a superficial involvement which reduces stewardship life to organizational aspects and often misguided goals. It seems to conform to Biblical concepts, but it is a counterfeit of the real thing. It is no answer or solution to the Biblical question of sanctification.

Conformity to a program replaces individual initiative and creativity. There is increased dependence on formalities and less on living faith shown in love. It is self-imposed spiritual poverty.

Approach Two

The supply-side approach emphasizes relationships — to God, to fellowmen, and to material possessions. It stresses spiritual growth, Christian fruits based on resources, and has $$ as a by-product. It is based on the calling or vocation in Christ. It stresses "who you are" before stressing "what you do."

The fullness of God's supply is: Grace — saved by it; Power —

kept by it; The Word — strengthened and guided by it; Providence — fed by it; Care — preserved by it; His Arms — held by them; Goods — humanly enriched by them. God is full of resources. He is all you need. He is faithful and more dependable than you or I. God can do everything but fail. God is worth our denial of things that harm us.

God is extravagant. He could have created a more modest universe. Why make billions of stars that can't be seen? His practice is to be liberal with His blessings. He spared nothing of His artistry in the Creation or of His love in the New Creation. The Cross is the epitome of extravagance. Truly, He is a big spender. But He is not a mindless spendthrift, for He does not give merely because we desire it. Sometimes He withholds, as any good father does.

Approach Two is concerned with *being* before *doing*, living in the grace of God before seeking to do the will of God. Its concerns are spiritual before they are financial.

Supply-Side Stewardship frees us from self-interest. It focuses on giving rather than receiving. It is not entangled in worldly affairs, but wholly absorbed in the Christian pursuit. There is a recognized need for constant spiritual nourishment. Workers need not be ashamed. Approach Two encourages living the faith in a spirit of love by the Spirit's power.

The supply-side approach provides complete security and hope through Christ's love and forgiveness. Being rooted in Christ and complete in Him, God's promises assure protection and safety.

This grace approach leads to true servanthood.

Steps to Take Now

This means that, wherever appropriate, we change:

1. *From* stewardship aimed at increase in contributions *to* stewardship education for strengthening spiritual life and fruitfulness;

2. *From* church gifts for meeting church bills *to* a stress on worshipful living wherein each person brings his life and substance to the altar;

3. *From* budget pressures *to* orderly planning and budgeting of resources;

4. *From* pledges of amounts *to* firstfruit, proportionate giving;

5. *From* giving measured by mathematical averages *to* giving measured by one's potential participation in ministry and mission;

6. *From* concern with $$ and service for the church *to* growing discipleship for everyone.

The difference between the maintenance and the supply-side models is the same as the difference between the sight dimension and the faith dimension (2 Cor. 3, 4, 5):

Sight Dimension	*Faith Dimension*
Letter	Spirit (3:6)
Ministry of Death	Ministry of Spirit (3:7–8)
Ministry of Condemnation	Ministry of Righteousness (3:8–9)
Darkness	Light (4:6)
Outer Man	Inner Man (4:16)
Seen	Unseen (4:18)
Temporal	Eternal (4:18)
Mortality	Life (5:4)
Outward Appearance	Heart (5:12)
Sinful Flesh	Man in Christ (5:16–17)

What we sometimes thought was freedom was actually bondage. As we consider the change from maintenance to supply side, we should consider the "World Civilizations Cycle," which is valid also in the Christian life and life-style: From bondage the cycle goes on to spiritual life, faith, courage, liberty, abundance, selfishness, complacency, apathy, dependence, and back to bondage. Where on this scale or cycle are you? Where is your church as an institution?

The key is balance between faith, courage, and liberty in that cycle. In order to maintain a balance, we need to recognize the barriers to a healthy sanctification and apply the Biblical truths and principles with integrity.

We get caught up on more and more activities, seeking more and more human solutions to the problems of life and the church. But those solutions only uncover a wider range of problems. In our quest to keep up with all our activities, we become more and more materialistic, which only adds to our problems. We burn out just trying to keep up the pace of church work. Often we are in disarray, wondering how we are going to get things under control.

Bureaucracy seems to be the order of the day. These bureaucracies are faceless giants controlled by some unseen "they" who carry out their desires in spite of all we do. So we watch as matters become less and less manageable.

The barriers include our busy lives compounded by many church meetings and often the clubhouse nature of our churches, sometimes even a ghetto existence. Sometimes there is a lack of vision, of motivation, or of a burden for the lost. A Biblical shallowness results in craving for status and success, manifested in authoritarian styles.

Sometimes the professionalizing of the clergy and of ministry rather than the equipping of the laity to use all their gifts is the problem, which tends to trivialize the great plan of God. Thus we measure the success of the church by the number of dollars in the church treasury. If you doubt this, ask yourself when a church gets real panicky. It is not when they have only 40% to 50% of their people at worship, only 20% or less in Bible study, and 5% to 10% witnessing, but they panic when the budget is not met. That is the real tip-off related to priorities and the confusion of ends and means.

Congregations experience greater loss than money—loss of people to whom they should be ministering. If the members focus on ministry, they will be strengthened for giving—by first overcoming spiritual weaknesses that are the cause of money shortages. People's life-style should be as great a concern as support for the church.

In the meantime we specialize in printing budget needs in every bulletin, print "scandal sheets," and encourage people to "give your fair share" and to "give until it hurts." We conduct bazaars when we should be teaching and equipping the saints for ministry, put memorials with people's names on everything they give, and make a big thing about barely meeting the bills. We find the youth and schoolchildren selling anything from candy bars, knick-knacks, candles, and fruit to pay for basic items like gym supplies for the school. We repeatedly work up a new program for a "quick fix."

We might as well follow the example of the pastor who during a congregation's financial crisis put it straight to the people one Sunday morning as he opened his stewardship sermon with this legalism, "I've always been wanting to say it, and today I will: You've got it, we need it, so give it!" Don't be shocked that an orthodox pastor would say this, for it is consistent with the frequent perversion of grace in our general stewardship practices.

We have been displaying some of the attributes of the Pharisees without intentionally being Pharisees. We fence in the church with rules, thinking that these will help. We are afraid of Christian freedom, and find it frightening. We abhor the word "Pharisee," but we want what they offer — a comfortable religious fraternity regimented by control mechanisms and a routine of religious uniformity and formalism.

This model stunts the creation of new ministries; indeed, it increases the likelihood of members working at a job, not in a ministry. It decreases the chances of the church responding to changing needs, emphasizing the *status quo* (which, facetiously, is Latin for "the mess we're in") and inhibiting change. It perpetuates a limited "power circle" in the church and restricts ownership by members. It successfully creates a stalemate of those few who desire pure Christian motivation and strategies against all those who cannot fathom the stewardship life under grace.

So we react to challenges by giving excuses for our stewardship behavior, mistakenly assuming that our stewardship performance is excusable. Instead of excuses, we need to let God move our congregation from maintenance to mission. This means that enthusiasm will replace passivity, corporate focus on grace goals will replace goallessness, a Great Commission direction will replace aimless drift, unity of purpose will replace divisiveness, and a true mission mentality will replace the maintenance mentality.

The supply side keeps the focus on value in contrast to cost. While maintenance is impressed mostly with cost, supply side seeks to keep a proper perspective on the value of the thing or activity under consideration. We should be more concerned with the value than with the price tag. Many know the price but not the value.

When confronted with an area of our life and of our church that might have to change, we will humble ourselves before God, having an attitude of mind and heart that is completely open to the Lord. Some will be changing life-styles, reducing their appetites, buying smaller cars and homes, changing jobs, always refusing to attach their self-image to status. Through perseverance we will take God at His Word.

CHAPTER THREE

THE FLOW OF GOD'S SUPPLY— CHRIST'S BODY IN ACTION

Stewardship is a life-style, a process, not a program. The life-style is dictated to us by God, that we may become functioning members of the body of Christ in the world. We are not just like the Body; we *are* the Body.

Questions about stewardship lead us straight to the heart of the Gospel, for the Gospel will influence what we say and do in our stewardship practices. Grace restores us to faithful stewardship. True life is a response to the Gospel, which restores us to God's purpose for life.

When we invent our own purposes, which seem so respectable, and substitute our will for the Creator's will, He still remains faithful to us rebels. We are raised with Christ in His resurrection to high purpose. Grace first points to the purpose of human life, then to how we can get what we need in order to fulfill that purpose. When we allow idols to survive, we lack the power to achieve what is required or to enjoy what we get. Grace liberates us from our own notions of stewardship, our idolatries and legalisms. Grace cancels man's stewardship regulations, but gives us God's purpose and power through the Gospel. Thus life in its totality is stewardship—a response to the Gospel.

Being Right with God—Justification

Christ's righteousness is now our righteousness. Our justification by grace through faith in Jesus Christ is complete, and it needs neither increase nor repetition. We are called saints because we are baptized into and justified by Christ, delivered from all our guilt and given a new relationship with God. This can never be gained by self-denial methods. Involved are five words: grace, man, God, Christ, and faith.

Grace tells us that heaven is a free gift. It cannot be earned or deserved. It is unmerited love.

Man is a sinner, and he cannot save himself.

God is merciful and just. He is merciful and does not want to punish us. But He is just, and He must punish sin. Unless we see the justice and love of God in true perspective, we don't understand Him or know Him.

God's compassion flows out of His goodness. Goodness without justice is not goodness. God spares us because He is good, but He could not be good if He were not just. So, justice is satisfied when God sends His Son to die to save us. As the holy God, He does not conform to our standard, for He Himself is that standard. Whatever belongs to God must be thought of as holy.

God rejects every attack on His sole rights as Lord. God's wrath is His necessary and proper stance toward all who oppose Him. He will not allow any being to take His place, nor anyone to take precedence over Him. God must destroy the unholy or else purge out the sin.

Christ is the infinite God-man, who paid for our sins by His death on the cross, purchasing abundant life for us here on earth and eternal life in heaven. This He offers as a gift that we may receive by faith. Faith is not mere intellectual assent or an earthly set of beliefs, but is trust in Jesus Christ alone for salvation, worked in us by the Holy Spirit.

This is reality, the inner circle of our lives, the basis for the world view of the Christian.

Richard F. Lovelace writes: "Only a fraction of the present body of professing Christians are solidly appropriating the justifying work of Christ in their lives. Many have so light an apprehension of God's holiness and of the extent and guilt of their sin that consciously they see little need for justification, although below the surface of their lives they are deeply guilt-ridden and insecure. Many others have a theoretical commitment to this doctrine, but in their day-to-day existence they rely on their sanctification for justification, in the Augustinian manner, drawing their assurance of acceptance with God from their sincerity, their past experience of conversion, their recent religious performance or the relative infrequency of their conscious, willful disobedience. Few know enough to start each day with a thoroughgoing stand upon Luther's platform: *You are accepted,* looking outward in faith and claiming the wholly alien righteousness of Christ as the only ground for acceptance, relaxing in that quality of trust which will produce increasing sanctification as faith is active in love and gratitude."[1]

Showing that the vigor and power of the spiritual life depend upon the mortification of sin, Lovelace states that true Christianity "has always come from its keenness in penetrating defense mechanisms, uncovering hidden sin and leading people—Christians and unbelievers alike—to repentance. . . . These tools must not be employed to move people once more into obedience to cultic legal codes. To maintain their spiritual vigor and to carry out their mission properly, Christians must be removed from the training devices of legalism and allowed to walk as those liberated by the work of the Cross, freed from human regulations and entrusted to the communion of the Holy Spirit who guides believers through the application of Biblical principles and precepts."[2]

Unless we understand our real humanity and our pretense of goodness, we will be caught in the outer circle of behavior or culture Christianity. Gradually we will be defining our stewardship traditions as rationally defensible and not recognize that we are legalistic moralists. As the nonbeliever accepts a whole universe of lies about creation and the world, so traditionalist Christians will embrace the stewardship delusion. We will have a whole reservoir of unrecognized, disordered motivation and stewardship response. We will continue to frame false images of ourselves and of God. We will be satisfied with a works religion which places an unbearable burden on our conscience because of the Biblical light we have. Such a conscience is forced to draw back into the twilight of self-deception. Either it manufactures a fictitious righteousness in heroic works of piety or it redefines sin in shallow terms so that it can lose the consciousness of God's presence and will. The distinction between justification and sanctification is blurred or lost.

Then we will assume that all church members are justified, whether or not they show evidence of conversion and sanctification. And so it follows that we project a softened image of God, minimizing His holiness and justice while maximizing His love, while Christ is more a motto than One with whom we have a close relationship. So our Christian convictions cool off and we move in the direction of subtle rationalism.

History has shown that the doctrine of justification is the key to spiritual release, letting the Christian see the radical depth of sin and the radical nature of grace. Justification is the basis for the genuine work of spiritual renewal. But our stewardship practices have given us a relapse into the old ways. We have sometimes succeeded in turning justification into dead orthodoxy with a one-sided emphasis on justification while neglecting sanctification and the proper use of the Law, including its third use. Such a procedure produces what Bonhoeffer called "cheap grace." Thus we have what some have called a "half-Reformation," which has reformed our doctrines but not our lives. Justification should release the blocked energy caused by "maintenance stewardship."

Sin and Guilt

Sin affects the Christian's life, will, and witness, weakening his love and restricting his liberty.

Since sin is a broken relationship and fellowship, a broken Law, it produces a broken life. Sin is present and the Law works whether we understand it or not. God's law is designed to direct us in the proper use of our bodies, minds, and spiritual lives for good stewardship. Refusals to submit are rebellion and insubordination. God has not given commandments to destroy us or even to inhibit the expression of our creative nature, but to guide us to harmonious relationships and the proper use of all of God's creation.

Sin affects the whole nature of man, and it causes us to abuse God and our fellowman. It causes life to be hollow and unreal. It is a destructive force. While we may be intellectually capable of good stewardship acts, sin makes us morally incapable.

Sin is the drug of drugs. Small tastes of sin eventually create an appetite for more and more until our life is twisted, bent, deformed, and perverted from what the regenerated life is meant to be. Only by getting to the root cause of our trouble— sin—can the storm of life be calmed and can we sail in the direction our new man wants to go.

Whereas we were made to enjoy life, guilt causes us only to endure it. Nothing we can do will atone for our sin or remove our guilt. Our tendency is to distract our attention temporarily from guilt or repress it chemically. Through forgiveness God made man free from guilt in order that he might enjoy God and life.

This moves us on to the vital subject of repentance and forgiveness, essential for better stewardship.

Repentance and Forgiveness

Judson Cornwall writes: "Repentance should become as common to the Christian as breathing. We exhale the bad and inhale the good. We will breathe out repentance and breathe in forgiveness. We will rid ourselves of inward sin and receive, as the reverse and subsequent action, the righteousness of God."[3] The greater our love for God, the quicker we will repent. Repentance precedes forgiveness. It prepares the repentant Christian to receive forgiveness. It means "to change one's mind." Repentance involves both a turning from sin and a turning to God.

Repentance first produces an intellectual adjustment, then an act of the will, and finally triggers deep emotional impulses toward action. We are to do works that show our repentance (Acts 26:20).

Forgiveness is a promise of the Father, a provision of the Son, a proclamation of the Spirit in the Word, and a required practice in the church. Forgiveness is part of the nature of God, not just a mood now and then.

Forgiveness restores us to a harmonious relationship with God. As children of God by grace we dare no longer carry a load of guilt that produces anxiety, destroys our zest for life, or hinders our service to God, for Jesus paid it all. Our sins have been paid for, and there is no condemnation against us. Jesus has blotted out the charges against us (Col. 2:14). God does not forgive and then file it away for future reference, but He erases the record.

Forgiveness not only means guilt removed but also gives inner healing and provides the strength to do stewardship acts. We need to accept forgiveness from God and then forgive ourselves, followed by the forgiveness of others. Our forgiving one another is not a payment to God assuring us of personal forgiveness, but it is a command to be obeyed. Forgiven ones make good forgivers. What God has given us through forgiveness He expects us, by His Spirit, to give to others.

Repentance and forgiveness lead to true freedom. We no longer need a "siege mentality," as though we are entrenched against the world and live an embattled life. We are now free to get out of our spiritual fortress and into the fray of life. True Christian freedom comes from knowing that God's forgiveness immunizes us against *slavery* to sin and we no longer need to worry about "catching" it. Now we are "carriers" of righteousness and expect to infect others with it. Maintenance stewardship keeps us enslaved in the fortress. Supply-side stewardship finds us stepping out into freedom. No longer in spiritual exile, we can now enjoy the excitement of God's grace in the stewardship of life.

Judson Cornwall says: "Let us enjoy forgiveness. We have been restored to a whole new life. Let's live it. . . . Let's stop punishing ourselves trying to 'help God out' but start enjoying our release from sin's penalty, pollution, power and guilt. We have been justified; let's enjoy it. In Christ we have been sanctified; let's savor it to the fullest. We are being glorified; let's delight in it. Let's stop listening to our memory circuits, and reprogram our minds to enjoy our new status as forgiven and loved people.

"The handcuffs have been removed. Rejoice!
The contract has been canceled. Sing!
The debt has been paid. Shout!
God's love has triumphed over His Law. Enjoy it!
Let's enjoy forgiveness!"[4]

Sanctification (Living for Christ)

The Gospel proclaims through the Word and sacraments a

free promise of grace made available by an act of God in the atonement of Jesus Christ, after which follows a life of sanctification.

Adolph Koeberle writes: "Faith that does not heed nor use this divinely-given gift of renewal perishes through its self-imposed poverty." He continues: "The paradox of God's sole activity and man's responsibility which is found in sanctification, as well as in justification, brings with it an entirely new conception of the New Testament imperatives whose importance and frequent occurrence cannot be emphasized strongly enough. . . . The numberless exhortations of the Epistles are actually addressed to those who are baptized, to the regenerate and to those who have become members of Christ in His Church, who on the basis of their communion with Christ already possess what is being required of them. . . . Since God has turned tasks into gifts in the Gospel, the believer can understand and accept such great things."[5]

The Spirit's regeneration leads to service and work for God (Eph. 2:1 – 10). The steward who does not understand who he is in God's plan and what his resources are will not know how to function properly. The steward should realize that God gives more than He demands. What God demands He first gives. That is a great encouragement for sanctification.

Throughout this book we emphasize that the Christian life is impossible without the power of the Holy Spirit, whose role in our call and its fulfillment needs to be properly understood. We cannot call ourselves to make decisions on our own about our work in the Kingdom. The Holy Spirit gives strength to be obedient to the call. The Spirit gives what God commands.

Sanctification is not saying, "Thank You, God, for getting me this far; now I'll take it on my own." It is not a bad person trying to be good, but an ill person seeking with God's help to be strong for service. That is the sinner-saint conflict, the Old Man-New Man civil war.

Through my consultations and seminars throughout North America and overseas I have learned the sad fact that the majority of Christians do not have a working knowledge of the New Man over the Old Man. This means that they don't really know who they are. We need to renew this understanding, a subject which has been fully covered in the book *Christian Stewards—*

Confronted and Committed.

If we are to live the truly sanctified and victorious life, we need to know about our addictions and how to overcome them. After visits and fellowship with a number of recovering alcoholic Christians and their families who are involved in Alcoholics Anonymous and Al-Anon, I have come to the conclusion that all of us are addicted to something, someway, somehow. There are food-aholics, choc-aholics, soft drink-aholics, spend-aholics, jog-aholics, car-aholics, tv-aholics, work-aholics, computer-aholics, greed-aholics, gossip-aholics, nicotine-aholics, caffeine-aholics, sugar-aholics, curse-aholics, sex-aholics, ski-aholics, pride-aholics, complain-aholics, envy-aholics, selfish-aholics. How many more need we name? The important thing is that we overcome these addictions and that we become recovering ". . . aholics," whatever our addiction may be.

The 12 steps of Alcoholics Anonymous provide wise and true direction for every Christian to take for better stewardship life.

The Twelve Steps of Alcoholics Anonymous

1. We admitted we were powerless over alcohol—that our lives had become unmanageable.
2. Came to believe that a Power greater than ourselves could restore us to sanity.
3. Made a decision to turn our will and our lives over to the care of God as we understood Him.
4. Made a searching, fearless moral inventory of ourselves.
5. Admitted to God, to ourselves, and to another human being the exact nature of our wrongs.
6. Were entirely ready to have God remove all these defects of character.
7. Humbly asked Him to remove our shortcomings.
8. Made a list of all persons we had harmed, and became willing to make amends to them all.
9. Made direct amends to such people wherever possible, except when to do so would injure them or others.
10. Continued to take personal inventory and when we were wrong, promptly admitted it.
11. Sought through prayer and meditation to improve our conscious contact with God as we understood Him, praying only

for knowledge of His will for us and the power to carry that out.

12. Having had a spiritual awakening as the result of these steps, we tried to carry this message to alcoholics and to practice these principles in all our affairs. (Reprinted with permission of AA World Services, Inc.)

Twelve Steps and Twelve Traditions[6] is an excellent resource for the reader. We will change the steps slightly to make them appropriate for our situation.

Step One: We admit we are powerless over our addiction—that our lives have become unmanageable. We must accept responsibility for our addictions or sinful habits, no matter how small, trivial, or insignificant in our own eyes. We need to own our own mistakes; do not blame others. Admission of powerlessness is the first step to freedom and liberation. There is a close relation between humility-repentance and overcoming addictions.

Step Two: The Holy Spirit has caused us to believe that only a Power greater than ourselves (the Triune God, Father, Son and Holy Spirit) can restore us to sanity. Our roadblocks are indifference, prejudice, intellectuality, self-sufficiency, defiance, and negative thinking. A right relation with God is imperative.

Step Three: By the Spirit's direction and power we have turned our will and our lives over to the care of God through forgiveness in Jesus Christ. This is like opening a locked door. Willingness and openness to God is the key. Dependence on God is the means to independence and freedom from addiction. We will avoid the misuse of will-power. The Holy Spirit's power in the Word is instrumental.

Step Four: We have made a searching and fearless moral inventory of ourselves. Here we discover our liabilities and recognize the extremes in our human and instinctive drives. A misguided moral inventory can result in guilt, blaming others, or playing games. Self-justification is dangerous. Willingness to take inventory, recognize sins and weaknesses, and to repent gives new confidence. This is the beginning of a life-time practice. Common symptoms of emotional insecurity are worry, anger, self-pity, and depression. This inventory reviews relationships. It must be thorough.

Step Five: We have admitted to God, to ourselves, and to

another human being the exact nature of our wrongs. This is a necessary deflation of ego in order to overcome addiction and to gain peace of mind. Confession is an ancient discipline, and it is grounded in the Holy Scriptures. Without fearless admission of defects, few could keep free from addictions. Now we lose our sense of isolation, receive assurance of forgiveness, and also give it. We learn humility, as we are honest and realistic about ourselves. We avoid rationalizing. This step leads to forgiveness and oneness with God and prepares us for the following steps.

Step Six: We are entirely ready to have God remove all these defects of character and actions. This is necessary for spiritual growth, and the beginning of a lifetime job. We will never be perfect human beings, but we need to strive as Paul encourages. Delay is dangerous, and rebellion may be fatal. This is the point at which we abandon limited objectives and move toward God's will for us.

Step Seven: We humbly ask God to remove our shortcomings. Here is true repentance and forgiveness in Christ, which is the avenue to true freedom of the human spirit. It is necessary for the survival of freedom. It is ego-puncturing and removes failure and misery. It exchanges strength for weakness. The pain of repentance is the admission price to the new life. It destroys self-centered fear. This changes our attitude and moves us out of ourselves toward God.

Step Eight: We make a list of all persons we have harmed, and are willing to make amends to them all. Living compatibly with others is a fascinating adventure. Obstacles to good personal relations are reluctance to forgive, failure to admit wrongs to others, and purposeful overlooking of our sinful acts. There is necessity for an exhaustive survey of the past related to the kind of harm done to others. This is the beginning of the end of isolation.

Step Nine: We make direct amends to such people wherever possible, except when to do so would injure them or others. Good timing is important to making amends. Peace of mind cannot be bought at the expense of others. There is a need for discretion. There must be readiness to take the consequences of our past and to take responsibility for the well-being of others.

Step Ten: We continue to take personal inventory and when we are wrong, we promptly admit it. Can we keep away from our addiction and keep our emotional balance under all conditions? Self-searching becomes a regular habit. We admit, accept, and patiently correct our defects. When the past is settled, present challenges can be met. Remember what leads back to addiction: anger, resentment, jealousy, envy, self-pity, and pride. Self-restraint is the first objective. All of this is insurance against trying to play the role of the "big shot." Look at credits as well as debits.

Step Eleven: We seek through prayer and meditation to improve our conscious contact with God, praying only for knowledge of His will for us and the power through the Spirit to carry it out. Meditation in God's Word and prayer are the main channels for keeping in touch with God. This is an unshakable foundation for life. Daily petitions are made for understanding God's will and for the grace to do it. There are rich rewards.

Step Twelve: Having had a spiritual awakening as the result of these steps, we try to carry this message to others who are addicted (whether to great or small things) and to practice these principles in all of life. "Joy of Living" is the theme of this step. Action is its key word. Giving is done without seeking a reward. There is love without a price tag. All is accepted as a free gift of God. Readiness to receive this free gift lies in the practice of these 12 steps. This is magnificent reality in the inner being.

Don't specialize in just eight or ten of the steps, but adopt "12-stepping" in demonstration of the faith. Growing spiritually is the solution to our problems. Place spiritual growth first above all else. There is to be a change in our outlook on material matters. Our instincts are to be restored to their true purpose. Understanding and faith are the keys to right attitudes, right actions, and good living.

These 12 steps will aid us in ridding ourselves of unwanted and unneeded additions, such as what Erma Bombeck calls the "lust to dust" syndrome. That means things you cannot live without—until you get them. When you get them, you enjoy them for awhile and often they are relegated to a secondary interest. In fact, what you lusted for is now gathering dust, despite all the sacrifice in time, energy, and money you may have spent to get it! What was most important at one time has now lost its significance. The Twelve Steps help you get everything into perspective.

Taking these steps will assure that our spirits will be filled with penitence, with no room for pride; our minds with truth, with no room for hypocrisy; our souls with peace, with no room for spite; our lives with grace, with no room for petty things.

Now that we have stated these steps in the present tense, we will keep repeating them in the past tense as recovering "... aholics" or addicts to one thing or another. We are on a path that really takes us somewhere, where life is not a dead end or something to be endured, but an adventure to be mastered by the transformation of the Spirit through Christ.

"Freely you have received, freely give" is the essence of these steps from a Christian viewpoint. Setbacks can become stepping-stones to greater things. There will be spiritual growing pains. We are growing from babes to maturity. Sometimes things can be disappointingly dull. We will not use any gift for our own destruction.

Sanctification is by God's grace a response to God's grace. The nature of human beings is that we are both morally responsible and free, not coerced but invited into doing obedience. Human response is impossible outside a context of authority and spiritual power. We believe this because God has revealed it, more in the indicative than in the imperative. All this rings true because of the Gospel. Truths are ultimately made relevant by decisions which make our faith functional through expression and firm commitments.

Justification—Sanctification (Position—Practice)

John MacArthur Jr. in his *Shepherdology* course reminds us how Ephesians tells the position (chs. 1–3) and practice (chs. 4–6) of life in the Body.[7]

Justification	Sanctification (Christian living)
Position (Unchanging)	Practicc (Changing and Growing)
1. Spiritually alive to God: Eph. 2:1, 4–5; 1 John 4:9; John 11:25	1. Live the Christian life (express the faith): Phil. 1:21; Gal. 2:20; Titus 2:12; Col. 3:2

2. Dead to sin: 1 John 1:9; Rom. 6:11	2. Give no place to sin: Rom. 6:11; Col. 3:2
3. Fully and freely forgiven: Eph. 1:7; 1 John 1:9; 1 John 2:12	3. Count on it! (Keep assured!): Rom: 8:1, 33–34
4. Righteous: Rom. 1:17; 3:21–26; 4:6	4. Live righteously: 2 Tim. 2:22; 1 John 3:7
5. Children of God: Eph. 1:5; Gal. 3:26	5. Act like God's children: Eph. 5:1; 1 Peter 1:13–14
6. Heirs of God: Rom. 8:17; Col. 1:12; Eph. 1:11, 14	6. Add to your inheritance: Matt. 6:19–21; 2 Cor. 5:9–10
7. Blessed with all spiritual blessings in the heavenly places: Eph. 1:3; 2:6–7; 2 Peter 1:3–4	7. Set your love on things above: Col. 3:1–2
8. Heavenly citizenship: Phil. 3:20; John 17:14–16; 1 John 5:4	8. Live as a citizen of heaven: 1 John 2:15; Col. 3:1–2; James 1:27
9. Servant of God: 1 Cor. 7:22; Rom. 6:22	9. Act like a servant: Rom. 6:17–19; 12:11; Heb. 12:28
10. New life: 2 Cor. 5:17	10. Walk in the new: life Rom. 6:4
11. Free from Law: Rom. 6:14; 7:4–6	11. Yet keep fulfilling the Law (third use): Gal. 5:1, 13–14; Rom. 8:4
12. Crucified to the world: Gal. 1:4; 6:14	12. Avoid worldly things: 1 John 2:15–17; James 4:4; Rom. 12:2
13. Light of the world: 1 Thess. 5:5; Matt. 5:14	13. Walk as children of light: Eph. 5:8; Matt. 5:15–16
14. Victorious over Satan: Rev. 12:9–11	14. Claim your victory (live victoriously): Eph. 6:11–17; James 4:7
15. Holy and without blame: Eph. 1:4; 1 Cor. 3:17	15. Live holy lives: 1 John 3:7; 1 Peter 1:15; 2 Peter 3:14
16. Free: John 8:32	16. Enjoy your freedom: Gal. 5:1
17. In Christ: Eph. 1:3, 10; 2:6, 13	17. Abide in Him: 1 John 2:28
18. Secure in Christ: 1 Peter 1:5; Rom. 8; John 10:27–29	18. Enjoy that security: Rom. 8:28
19. One with Christ and Christians: Eph. 4:4–6; 1:9–10	19. Live that oneness: Eph. 4:3; John 17:21, 24
20. In grace: Rom. 5:1–2	20. Grow in grace: 2 Peter 3:18
21. In fellowship: 1 Cor. 1:9; 1 John 1:3–7	21. Experience that fellowship: Rev. 3:20

22. Indwelt and led by the Spirit: 1 Cor. 6:19; Rom. 8:9, 14
22. Yield to the Spirit's control: Eph. 5:18; 4:30; 1 Thess. 5:19

23. Spirit-gifted: 1 Cor. 12:7, 11; Eph. 4; Rom. 12:6a
23. Use your gift: Rom. 12:6–8; 1 Peter 4:11

24. Empowered for service: Acts 1:8; Eph. 3:20; 2 Cor. 4:7
24. Claim and demonstrate that power: 1 Cor. 2:4; Phil. 3:10; Eph. 6:10; Phil. 4:13

25. Received love: Rom. 5:5; 1 John 2:5
25. Love! 1 Peter 1:22; 4:8; John 13:34; 1 John 3:18

Functioning as Christ's Body

God has fitted us and holds us together as members of Christ's body for service to Him (Eph. 4:16). Service is based on the ability and work assigned to each member. Each member has supply from God to help build up others and to do all of God's work. See how much God has built interdependence into the working of the church, His body, and how much we are dependent upon each other. But the Body is crippled because ordinarily 60% or 70% of the members just sit in pews and do not function according to God's purpose.

How is this edifying possible for each member? It happens because Christ is the Head, who gives us forgiveness and who speaks to us through His Word. "To each one of us grace was given according to the measure of Christ's gift" (Eph. 4:7). He provides pastors and teachers to equip "the saints for the work of ministry, for the edifying of the body of Christ, till we all come to the unity of the faith and the knowledge of the Son of God, to a perfect man, to the measure of the stature of the fullness of Christ" (Eph. 4:12–13). We are no longer to be little children spiritually but to grow in knowledge and faith.

We are to be capable of edifying, that is, to build each other up by speaking the Word of Law and the Word of Gospel to each other. Leaders are to encourage all members to discover, develop, and deploy their individual gifts or abilities. All are to be active in ministry.

Everyone is a steward or manager of God's gifts: "It is required in stewards (managers) that one be found faithful" (1 Cor. 4:2). God does not require us to be full of abilities or money, but full of faith. Such faith will lead us to obedience to the Great Commission.

The parable of the talents (Matt. 25:14–30) provides another dimension to our functioning in the Body. God is the Giver and has a right to recover what He has given and to receive dividends and interest. Ownership is not transferred to the user. God remains Lord and Master. So, the Christian is a manager of God's goods and is accountable to Him. God will entrust to us what is in our ability and not beyond it. What He asks for, He first supplies. The gifts differ, but each is to gain dividends. God expects multiplication out of the assets He shares, not just maintenance. He expects returns and commends the faithful investors. He gives advancement and increased gifts to the faithful. He strongly disapproves of neglect of duty and laziness, taking away the gift from one who refused His management and made excuses.

The Master's interests are placed completely in the steward's hands, as he is trusted with property, business, reputation, and plans. More than merely keeping the resources intact and preventing loss, the steward is to use them to enhance and enlarge his Master's interest. Thus, God's resources are to be increased for Him.

Trust Account Transfer

Our gifts from God can be called a *Trust Account* from Him, a term used by Jim Jackson. Our use of these gifts (stewardship or management of abilities, time, and money) to aid the needy or for the Gospel task of the church may be called a *Transfer*.

Thus, a stewardship act or service given through Christ's church or some charitable group for people in need is called a *Trust Account Transfer.*

What has God placed into our life and hands as our *Trust Account*? First, our physical life, and then our spiritual blessings, which center in the forgiveness of sins and the means of grace. Next, God has given us material blessings and relationships which help to enrich us and others in the body of Christ for service in the Kingdom.

God places into our *Trust Account* all these blessings from His storehouse of grace and love. When God promises: "I will bless you . . . and you shall be a blessing" (Gen. 12:2), it could be restated: "I will place spiritual, physical, material, mental, and relational gifts into your *Trust Account,* and you will be a blessing as you *Transfer* these to others."

Each of us has a God-given *Trust Account,* and we need to identify all that has been placed in it. We can recognize our gifts as we go through the following exercise:

AREA	TRUST ACCOUNT -God's Supply- -Intake-	TRANSFER -Suppliers (Our Trust)- -Output-
1. Spiritual	Salvation, Faith Baptism, Communion Word, Love	Confess, witness, edify.
2. Physical	Body, Time, Food, Strength	Eat moderately. Exercise. Keep fit.
3. Material	Home, Transportation, Possessions, Income, Estate	Give God generous firstfruits, then prioritize spending on family and other areas.
4. Abilities	Knowledge, Specific Abilities and Spiritual Gifts	Use them in various ministries in the church and to help fellowmen.
5. Relational	Relatives, Fellow Christians, Body of Christ	Edify, fellowship, disciple, exhort. Encourage.

Other Dimensions for Transfers

God expects us to exercise responsible stewardship of our *Trust Account* and to invest for accomplishing His purposes. This involves children, teens, young adults, mature adults, and retirees of all ages. Other than the *Transfers* stated above, here are additional ideas: visits, telephone calls, letters and cards to help those in various kinds of need. The need may be emotional, spiritual, physical, material, or incidental. Help can be given in the areas of spiritual need and of service, education, crafts, and transportation.

Whatever kind of service is required within the Body, the *Transfers* achieve three blessings: The need is met, thus blessing the recipient; good is done, blessing the donor; Christ is served, blessing the church and witnessing to the world.

What a plan God has for us! We get enriched by God and by

His people, and we enrich others by the use of God's gifts to us. No one can improve on that plan. We can only be disobedient to it.

Now fill out the *Trust Account Transfer* form for your own life. Write in what God has placed into your *Trust Account* from His storehouse, then write in how you are transferring that supply.

AREA	TRUST ACCOUNT -God's Supply- -Intake-	TRANSFER -Our Trust- -Output-
Spiritual		
Material		
Physical		
Abilities		
Relational		

Look for a special stewardship opportunity or the chance to make a *Trust Account Transfer* regularly, daily if possible, until it becomes part of your everyday life. You will be bringing strength, joy, and encouragement to others wherever you go. That's what life is all about, isn't it?[8]

CHAPTER FOUR
MORE THAN STEWARDS: SERVANTS

Because we inherited our stewardship practices through tradition as much as from the Bible, it is difficult for people to understand and practice being true servants of Christ. Due to the tyranny of the maintenance model, we have found it difficult to complete even the urgent institutional requirements. Most lay leaders are exhaustingly absorbed in the organizational rat race, which saps human resources.

What would be the result if the leaders and mass of lay people could be spiritually released from their slavery to the church systems and reoriented to be servants in the Biblical sense? Local and worldwide missions would be enriched with a new flow of personnel and resources needed for a whole variety of new ministries. Besides gaining each member as a student of the Bible, one of the chief goals of the congregation ought to be that each one becomes a servant. Yet the servant nature of Christianity is little known and practiced in the church.

The Scriptures show how important it is to be a true servant. When the disciples asked Jesus who would be the greatest in the kingdom of heaven, He took a child and said: "Unless you are converted and become as little children, you will by no means enter the kingdom of heaven. Therefore whoever humbles himself as this little child is the greatest in the kingdom of heaven" (Matt. 18:1–4). Simplicity and humility in life and practice make a great Christian.

The mother of Zebedee's children misunderstood this when she asked Jesus to grant that her two sons might sit on Christ's right and left hand in His kingdom. Jesus told them that they did not know what they were asking, and questioned whether they were able to drink of the cup that He was about to drink. They said, "We are able." They did not understand spiritual truths of greatness and did not realize that Jesus was referring to suffering necessary for gaining a position of honor. When they wanted to be "big shots," Jesus pointed them to servanthood. He said: "Whoever desires to be first among you, let him be your slave—just as the Son of Man did not come to be served, but to serve . . ." (Matt. 20:20–28).

John 13:3–5 is an astounding message of servanthood: "Jesus, knowing that the Father had given all things into His hands, and that He had come from God and was going to God, rose from supper and laid aside His garments, took a towel and girded Himself. After that, He poured water into a basin and began to wash the disciples' feet, and to wipe them with the towel. . . ." Note that the God-Man who had come from God and was going back to God, who had everything on earth in His hands, did not step up to a royal throne with royal clothes to preach a sermon or to receive the adulation of men. Rather, with a simple towel around Him, He washed and wiped the feet of His followers. Peter objected that Jesus would never wash his feet. However, only as He washed their feet could they have a part with Him. Servanthood is the true nature of the Christian faith.

Once when great multitudes followed Him from place to place, Jesus went away to a mountain and away from the popularity of the crowds, saying: "Blessed are the poor in spirit . . . those who mourn . . . the meek . . . the merciful . . . those who are persecuted" (Matt. 5:1–10). Resisting adoration by the crowds, He spoke of the humility and meekness of the Christian.

What do we learn from this? Our great efforts, our results, and our wealth are our poverty, while our true riches are a humble and contrite heart leading to selfless service. Once slaves of the flesh, now we are servants of God. If we want to be great, we should select some lowly individual or someone who hates us and go to them clothed with true humility to "wash their feet," that is, do some act of service and kindness.

This begins with accepting the mind-set and example of Jesus as seen in Phil. 2:1–11. We are not to look only for our own interests, but also for the interests of others. We should have the mind of Christ, who being in the form of God took the form of a servant, coming in the humble likeness of men to be obedient even to the death of the cross. The Exalted One was great because He was the humble and obedient Servant.

Therefore we do not strive for status positions, recognition, and power with self-serving motives. No task will be too small. In our humble servanthood we will bring glory to Him who called us. We will be totally oriented toward the One who gave the Great Commission. We will lose fear of failure or rejection, because victory is assured as Jesus makes intercession for us.

"God resists the proud, but gives grace to the humble. Therefore humble yourselves under the mighty hand of God, that He may exalt you in due time" (1 Peter 5:5–6). Donald Grey Barnhouse preached a sermon on this text, using the topic "The Way to Up Is Down; the Way to Down Is Up." If you want to be great, go down on your knees. Pastors and elders cannot fulfill their leadership roles adequately until the congregation sees them in the servant role.

Servanthood with deep compassion for the spiritual and physical needs of those in the Body and in the world who are hurting is the *support system* required in our day as in the time of Jesus. Few churches have the kind of support system needed today. Adding more stewardship programs and social ministry activities is inadequate. Servanthood is the only answer to the sickness and sin in the world.

A basic principle of servanthood is to give yourself away. You possess only what you have given away. Let the church give herself away at all levels, and watch her grow! Let members give themselves away, and watch the strength, joy, and peace! Servants will find no withdrawal or in-grownness. Rather, they will be willing to be vulnerable, run the risk.

The goal of this servanthood is not single activities, but obedience to Jesus, who said: "You shall love the Lord your God with all your heart, with all your soul, and with all your mind. . . . You shall love your neighbor as yourself" (Matt. 22:37–39). The loving servant is the link between Christ and the person in crisis.

Great care needs to be taken not to institutionalize our servanthood. While congregations need to build a network and a support system that are structured, nonstructured servanthood should not be inhibited or destroyed.

Servants in Service Activities

Most members of most churches seem to be merely existing with spiritual trimmings and participating in Christian ceremonies without evidence of actively pursuing service opportunities. When service is provided, it is more likely an involvement in occasional projects rather than a sustained servant life.

John Naisbitt, author of *Megatrends,* says that people everywhere are looking for commitment. The problem is that it is difficult for them to find activities that are sufficiently worthwhile and challenging in order to claim their commitment. Small church projects performed sporadically are not enough. Most situations allow people to hold on to their selfishness while they are performing the service. The revolutionary principle of servanthood begins with the death of self. Only those who have died to themselves will be true servants and serve others genuinely.

There are practical steps for this "self-death," which you can learn in Col. 3:5: "Put to death, therefore, whatever belongs to your earthly nature: sexual immorality, impurity, lust, evil desire and greed, which is idolatry" [NIV]. If we are to be obedient to Christ, we must mortify or put to death our old nature, which means to destroy the vitality and functioning of self. The Holy Spirit provides the strength for our minds to be remolded, our values renewed, our steps to take new paths.

Christians will not claim their freedom indiscriminately, but heed the words of Paul: " 'Everything is permissible for me'—but not everything is beneficial. . . . But I will not be mastered by anything. . . . Do it all for the glory of God" (1 Cor. 6:12; 10:31). We will avoid anything that puts us under sin's power. Bad habits must be broken—or we may find ourselves easily tolerating a sinful habit or using the "just one more time" excuse.

On the contrary, Paul says that we are to train or discipline ourselves to be godly (1 Tim. 4:7b), and he observes: "Everyone who competes in the games goes into strict training" (1 Cor. 9:25 NIV). This begins with a disciplined intake of God's Word that involves a planned time and a planned method. Obeying the

Scriptures, as Christ said, is also a discipline which requires a disciplined pattern of life.

Rom. 7 mirrors our struggle with sinful habits, telling us that we should take time for progress in knowing and practicing God's will. There is no such thing as instant godliness or holiness. Servants discipline themselves. As such, they learn to be "instruments of righteousness" (Rom. 6:13).

Christians as "instruments of righteousness" will discipline their use of time as God supplies it. Some are supplied with long life, some short, but all have the same amount—24 hours— every day. It cannot be hoarded or stretched. God expects us to use it wisely, to recognize its great value for service to Him and our fellowmen. Priorities should be established for time spent on work, family, recreation, and spiritual things.

People should be encouraged to learn how they are using their time now and be helped to recognize "time wasters," especially the inordinate time wasted by watching TV. This matter is a crucial issue today, since the stewardship of some people has been hampered by overindulgence in TV. This results in failure to serve the Lord adequately.

Service Possibilities for All

Have our programs emerged from the demands of institutional maintenance rather than responding to the need of the people to express their faith in Christian service? The maintenance approach causes us to accept too much from too few in the church. How will we use the fullest potential of most members?

Most of us are well acquainted with service opportunities as stated in the "Talents Enlistment Form" in *Christian Stewards Confronted and Committed,* pp. 181—82. We will not repeat the list of service opportunities, such as holding officer positions in the congregation and its organizations.

We advise that the word "volunteer" not be used in seeking the commitment of abilities on the part of members. We are not really seeking volunteers, since God has called each member to specific tasks on the basis of abilities given (Eph. 4). Since these members did not choose Jesus, but Jesus chose them "to go and bear fruit—fruit that will last" (John 15:16 NIV), they are to be challenged to discover their abilities and spiritual gifts, and to use them.

The congregation will produce a clear mission statement of service on the part of the members, helping them to identify their abilities and spiritual gifts, to match these abilities with service opportunities, and to fit and grow into their ministries. The church will train them, support them, and give them positive evaluations. The congregation and the church at large will develop new ministries that result from the pool of "talent resources" offered by the gifted people. Many workers will expand ministries to the sick, orphaned, widowed, imprisoned, unemployed, and those who have experienced a catastrophe.

Members will be aided in understanding this matter of making proper commitments as they are led through the "Trust Account Transfer" form. This was presented in ch. 3. After presenting this to your members, you will want to supply a blank form for them to work out for their own lives and situations.

Begin by asking all participants to write down in the "Trust Account" or "God's Supply" column what gifts God has given them in each of the categories. After that is completed, ask them to go to the right column, "Transfer," and write down how they are regularly transferring or using these gifts of God. It would be well to provide the *Trust Account Transfer* tract and also provide *Trust Account Pads* for members to get into the habit of making *Trust Account Transfers*.

There are two age groups of members which need more attention: the retirees and the youth or teens. Everyone needs to be reminded that the call to servanthood and service is for life, from childhood to the day of our death.

Service Opportunities for Retirees

No one retires or drops out from God's service at the age of 65. John 9:4 is not negated at age 70. Anyone who uses the excuse that he is retired in order to avoid Christian service to his Savior should be asked, "Retired from what? Have you retired from God? Has He retired from you? Are you still breathing and is your heart still beating? Is your mind still functioning? You will know when you are retired, for God will inform you by reason of poor health or by death."

Retirees are the most untapped resource in the church today! Various people have told us this at seminars we have conducted throughout our country. Retirees have larger blocks of discretionary time with flexibility of schedules than anyone else. True, productive retirees may be busier than ever because of their interests, but their work should involve a general Christian witness and, more specifically, blocks of time for servant activities.

Retirees have a life full of experiences, training, skills that have been mastered, mature personalities, and have nothing to prove. Activities that have purpose will help them keep their self-esteem. There will also be fringe benefits, such as having a satisfied and fulfilled life.

Retirees should be brought together as a group in order to minister and be ministered to. They have a ministry to the church and to each other. There should be some kind of structured organization. Let them choose their own leaders.

The first step is to utilize a "talent enlistment form" in order to help people identify their abilities and spiritual gifts. They can serve as a congregational officer, do research for the church office, supply services to the incapacitated, perform a telephone ministry, or make visits. They can conduct Bible classes in retirement homes, make evangelism calls or stewardship visits, supply transportation for those who have none, use their skills at retiree centers. There should be a sustained community among the retirees to provide support for one another and also for those outside the church.

Retiree groups should plan an active program with regular weekly meetings (not monthly, but weekly), with topics, speakers, Bible study, talent shows, and fellowship. They should offer recreation programs and activities, prayer groups and social gatherings. Tape-recorded services should be taken to shut-ins by retirees.

Trips may be arranged for those who have good health and can afford it. Neighboring congregations might plan together to arrange trips farther away.

The buddy system may be used, pairing more active individuals and couples with less active ones. This will be an encouragement for more to participate regularly and also serve to train others.

Excellent resource books for retiree ministries and servanthood are *Engaging the Aging in Ministry* (Bergman-Otte,

Concordia Publishing House) and *Aging Together—Serving Together: A Guide to Congregational Planning* (Augsburg).

Service Opportunities for Youth

A Kansas correspondent to "Dear Abby" suggested a creative and purposeful way of using the concept of "Walkathons" by youth. While she could not see the relation between charity and how far a person can walk, she saw real value if the youth were sponsored for performing a meaningful service. She suggested the following: Trashathon (How much litter can be picked off the streets, roads, and land?), windowathon (How many windows of senior citizens can be washed?), readathon (How many pages can be read to nursing home patients whose eyes have failed them?). More suggestions: writeathon (How many letters can be written for nursing home patients?), cleanathon (How many senior citizens' yards can be raked or otherwise cleaned up?). She asked why walkers should expend all that energy just to wind up with sore feet and aching muscles instead of using their energy for some worthwhile service, which we would call a servant opportunity, one that is both productive and charitable.

Helpful service may be provided for the church property: caring for the lawn, shoveling walks, planting and weeding flowerbeds, washing church and parish hall windows, repairing hymnals, etc. Toys could be collected and repaired for the church nursery or preschool.

Following these suggestions will give youth an opportunity to experience servanthood and be an encouragement to adopt this way of life for the rest of their time on earth.

The Servant's Care of His Body

While we have covered the matter of the body and health quite adequately in *Christian Stewards Confronted and Committed,* the subject needs review here in order to impress upon us the relation of the health of the servant and his service. True servanthood includes control over our physical bodies and appetites, which were created by God and are not sinful in themselves. If not controlled, our bodies can become "instruments of unrighteousness" (Rom. 6:13).

Michel Quoist writes: "If your body makes all the decisions and gives all the orders, and if you obey, the physical can effectively destroy every other dimension of your personality. Your emotional life will be blunted and your spiritual life will be stifled and ultimately will become anemic."[1]

When Paul urges us to present our bodies a living and holy sacrifice, acceptable to God, and not to be conformed to this world (Rom. 12:1–2), he reveals that God wants us to control our natural appetites and desires and avoid all overindulgences, including food. Do not miss Paul's point by considering this discipline or abstinence as legalistic; it is, rather, part of the obedience of faith. Our consumption of food and drink should be controlled by an awareness that our bodies are the temple of the Holy Spirit.

Far too often people look at such matters as negative restrictions, which take the fun out of life. The opposite is true: Usually they put joy back into life. The human body is a precious resource from God for productivity and enjoyment. This is the positive reason for obeying the will of God related to proper diet and exercise.

God has established principles which promote health. Bodily health greatly affects our productivity and work. Poor health adversely affects our job, our social life, our marriage, everything. There is a need for seeking dietary understanding and adopting eating and exercise habits that will build strong, vigorous bodies, helping us avoid sickness, disease, and physical weaknesses. We are responsible for the development and use of our bodies.

If there is a physical hereditary problem such as a coronary condition (some problems affect from 1% to 10% of people), then this must be recognized. Guilt must not be laid on any individual. However, even those physical problems are relieved considerably by good health habits.

Proper nutrition corrects many physical problems. Contributing to ill health, physical weakness, and cardiac problems are caffeine, excess sugar and salt, alcohol, smoking, and many drugs.

Regarding the smoking of cigarettes, various countries have now issued warnings that it is hazardous to health, as it limits and often destroys the physical condition a person should achieve. Particularly vulnerable are the unborn babies of pregnant women, as is also the case in drinking alcohol. The world's message through TV, radio, and newspaper advertisements is very strong, sometimes almost cruel, such as this one: "Stop smoking and losing; smokers are losers." This is a message from the *world,* not the church.

Where is the church in its warnings against the hazardous nature of cigarette smoking and overindulgence in other areas? The Christian's appropriate action regarding smoking should be:

1. Refrain from smoking yourself. It is not just the abuse but the use of cigarettes which is harmful.
2. Warn others about the harmful effects and encourage them to quit.
3. Refrain from leading others into this harmful habit by irresponsible remarks or example (especially true of parents, teachers, and pastors).
4. Be patient, understanding, and helpful to those who have developed the habit of smoking and find it difficult to break.

While negatives need consideration, our focus must be on positive health habits such as exercise. Various doctors, professors, and sports experts indicate that regular exercise is very helpful through:

1. Improved cardiovascular efficiency.
2. Increased blood supply to the heart muscle.
3. Reduction in body weight, in blood fats, blood pressure, and improved glucose tolerance.
4. Increased cellular sensitivity to insulin, reducing insulin requirements at any glucose level.
5. Reduction in elevated blood triglycerides and an increase in the amount of cholesterol carried by high density lipoproteins.
6. Improvement in other health habits, including better attention to proper diet and lessened desire to smoke.
7. Improved stress management.
8. Greater joy in living.

Since God is the Giver of life and health, the Christian will earnestly seek to avoid doing whatever needlessly destroys, harms, shortens, or endangers life and health. Since God in love created, redeemed, and regenerated us in order that we might live for Him and our fellowman, the Christian will earnestly endeavor to avoid whatever hinders him in service or shortens his time of service to God on earth. Since he is concerned not only with the eternal salvation of others but also with their full enjoyment of life on earth, the Christian will strive to avoid setting an example which might lead others into harmful habits which hinder and shorten their life and service to God.

Establish good eating habits, exercise regularly, avoid unnecessary stimulants, get enough sleep, and let your Christian faith give you strong and healthy emotions which will help you avoid fear and worry and an improper life-style filled with all kinds of harm and risks.

Leader for Health Habits

Lyle E. Schaller in an article in *Church Management— The Clergy Journal* asks, "Why Not a Minister of Health?"[2] He says that various congregations have been motivated to establish food pantries and clothing centers where those in need can receive food and clothing. Churches have a system of visiting those who are confined to a hospital or a nursing home. He writes, "Perhaps the next step should be to consider adding a nurse to the program staff of the congregation." Most congregations would possibly utilize an unpaid talent or one who serves part-time. In addition, there should be someone who is in charge of a committee on body and health.

Why do this? We would ask, why have we ignored it when it is so vital and so many people are violating their body and health? The Christian congregation is supposed to be concerned with the whole person, which includes the health business. Furthermore, there is an increasing recognition today of the value of preventative medicine or preventative steps. Most of all, the congregation is already involved in and concerned with the health of the parishioners through pastoral care, prayer, fellowship, and mutual support. Schaller says that this is simply expanding a current phase of ministry.

The health leader will concentrate on wellness, being healthy, not sick. The servant nature of Christianity suggests this step. It also suggests concern for pursuing God's principles of sex and of the sanctity of life, including the unborn. We can be sure that the God who knit us together in our mothers' wombs, and in whose book is written the forming of every part, cares intensely about the fate of the unborn (Ps. 139:13, 15–16). The Supplier of all, including children, will require an accounting for 55 million abortions worldwide each year. This is horrendous stewardship not only of human beings whose life and potential has been denied by selfish murder, but it also takes its toll on the physical and spiritual health of the prospective mothers. How ironic that the type of people who fight to save baby seals and the garter fish not only condone but promote the death of unborn human beings. What an abuse of God's supply, grace, and plan for the life of all. Christian stewards should be messengers of pro-life truths and activists who will glorify God and dignify man. Faithful stewardship on the part of such stewards suggests group endeavors to promote adoption into Christian homes as the alternative to abortion.

Servants Using Earthly Goods and Income

Faithful Christian servants know that the good life is not the life of acquisition and accumulation. They will be wary of the allurement and seductive power of things. The values within society are drugs that cause us to rationalize our materialistic life-style.

The subtle sin of materialism has created a delusion in the minds of many Christians that they can handle money simply by will power. They delude themselves because materialism is a subtle sin which usually does not come in the form of blatant and crass greed, but in almost unnoticeable ways. Indeed, a little "Jesus-veneer" is applied over our life-style, and consumerism becomes approved. Some Christians capitalize on the "health and wealth gospel" which makes them believe, "God wants me rich," "I deserve everything I've got." This leads to the determination that "I want what I want, and I want it now." Then it is only a step away to saying, "I am prospering; God must be pleased with me." They do not understand that whether we prosper or not, neither condition is necessarily a demonstration of God's pleasure or displeasure. Without realizing it, many people are owned by things even while they own their things. The things of God are placed at the periphery of their lives.

In a commencement address to Taylor University graduates, Charles Colson spoke of the decay in American Christianity and the need to challenge the prevailing values that are steadily taking root in religious communities. He observed that a Christian radicalism and revolutionary attitude is required to extricate ourselves from the notion that "money is the root of all good."

He pointed to the dreadful lie of money and materialism "in its promise of giving meaning to life, which it cannot provide." He said, "God does not demand our achievements; He demands our obedience."

We need to look at greed, its premise and perversity, and at God's prescription. The premise is that life does consist in the abundance of a person's possessions, contrary to Luke 12:15. Then the purpose of life is wrapped up in the needs of self. The incentive of life is to gain enough "stuff" for personal security and happiness. The rewards of life are to enjoy comfort and pleasure bought with our money.

The perversity of greed manifests itself in unbelief: there is a lack of faith that God will provide. There is little concern or responsibility for the neighbor's spiritual or physical needs. As we know from Christ's parables, the result of greed is unhappiness in this life and hell in the next.

God's prescription for greed is that we must not be foolish but rather see greed as being rich in goods but not in God (Luke 12:21). Having Jesus as Savior and Lord is the solution. Christ's love makes Him the ultimate Fulfiller of all our needs. People should be taught the dangers of loving money: The desire is never satisfied (Eccl. 5:10–11); the desire leads to "all kinds of evil" (1 Tim. 6:10); the desire causes discontentment (1 Tim. 6:6–7); the desire separates man from God (Matt. 6:24).

Greed also drives some people to gamble, to meet desires that cannot be met through earned income. Gambling and lotteries are get-rich-quick schemes, which are dangerous: Participants often risk money they cannot afford to lose; they make hasty decisions: they are at the mercy of chance; they lose much more often than they win.

The consequences of loving money are that we easily forget God, stop trusting Him, compromise Biblical principles, are deceived, become ungrateful and proud, and then rob God and others.

Money should not cause a Christian to worry (Matt. 6:25). It should not corrupt the Christian (Ps. 1:6), build up his ego (James 1:9–10), cause the Christian to hoard (Ps. 49:10–11), or be used to satisfy every whim and desire (1 Tim. 6:6–8).

Contentment

Money has much to do with character and contentment. Godly people who are content are very rich, whether they have much money or not. Thus some "rich" people have money and some do not. Money has little to do with either riches or poverty. The Laodiceans had lots of money, but they made the mistake of saying they were rich. But the Spirit said: No, you are poor and don't know it (Rev. 3:17). When Jesus suggested to the young man who had great possessions that he use his money to help the poor, he refused. By so doing, he kept his money and joined the ranks of the poor. That is why God says that godliness with contentment is "great gain" (1 Tim. 6:6).

Contentment does not come with ownership, but with the realization that God owns all. Contentment is not centered in the accumulation of things or in outward circumstances. If it were, we could gain greater contentment by moving up the street or down the road a little way to a bigger house, or take another job. If we "have to have it," we are not content. If wanting more is what makes us content, we will never be content.

Someone has said that "It is better to live content in a tent than to live with malice in a palace." Thirteen out of 15 Irish Sweepstakes winners who had become instant millionaires said they were more unhappy now than before they won the money. The problems of wealth, with increased anxiety, set in quickly. One Christian said that his acquisition of a prized possession gave him two happy days—the day he bought it and the day he sold it. It cost him much money every time he used it, and it cost him much when he didn't use it.

It is not the possessions that enslave us, but our attitude. How to be content with our possessions? First, concentrate on what you have, not on what you lack. Appreciate what you have. If you complain about your lack of wealth when you make a modest salary, you will also complain when you make a larger salary. Remember who serves whom. Possessions are our servants, not our masters. Don't buy anything you cannot afford, and avoid impulse buying. Don't buy things you can't use, that is, avoid just collecting. Develop the habit of sharing, and give God the first portion.

Contentment is related not only to money, but also to other

aspects of our life-style. Contentment has siblings: not only wise handling of money but also a balanced life-style and good health habits.

Financial Planning

Personal financial planning and money management is the responsibility of every Christian, yet the majority are poorly prepared to manage properly and effectively. The past decade has seen a great awakening to the necessity of providing information and training church members. Yet only a very small percentage of members are being touched, and so financial chaos continues to wreak its havoc on Christians, too. There is no chance for servanthood until people learn the Biblical principles. This begins with the recognition that internal enemies such as bad attitudes and habits are more powerful than the enemies outside us.

Where does the money go? It does not disappear in a hole or into the air, but leaves the hands of people when they are fully conscious. They spend it on a host of legitimate expenses and also waste far too much. Only when people start keeping records and compare spending and goals will they see that much of the money being spent does not actually help them. Sensible financial planning is the answer.

Financial planning involves "a plan for developing step-by-step where you are, what you have, what you need, and what needs to be done to reach wherever you want to go." The basic purposes are to conserve the capital you are earning, put you in control of your finances, help identify your financial problems, and give you confidence in the handling of your own finances.

The objectives are to make maximum use of your total income and each dollar, understand all alternatives, recognize warning signals and mistakes, adopt basic steps for budgeting, save, invest, avoid the debt trap, make a good estate plan, have a family awareness of the available income, give careful attention to spending, adopt a sensible life-style, and above all give generous, firstfruit offerings to the Lord.

Members should be helped to understand proper financial priorities and the rewards of being responsible. Christians will seek to avoid bondage to self-indulgences which lead to financial slavery. If we are to enjoy financial freedom, we need to have the contentment of mind which gives to God first, avoids pressure from bills, plans for adequate insurance and a good retirement plan. Such discipline frees rather than confines, stimulates rather than depresses. The reason is that God blesses obedience to His principles.

Needs must be separated from wants. Alexander Solzhenitsyn was quoted in a June 30, 1975, speech in Washington, D.C.: "Something which is incomprehensible to the human mind is the West's fantastic greed for gain which goes far beyond all reason, all limitations, and good conscience." This means that we must test the values which determine how our money will be spent. Our checkbook and credit card account will reveal much about our priorities and our relation with God.

The Servant Handling Wealth

How much is enough? While each person must answer that question for himself, the subject needs careful attention in the church. God does not require believers to give all their money away. However, the conscience of the rich needs to be alerted to the supreme obligation to do justice and right, which God has imposed by His gift of wealth committed to them.

What may one keep and spend upon oneself? God's Word seems to suggest: We may keep and use whatever we truly need for our calling, our task in the world. Easily beguiled into thinking that our wealth is all our own, we are faced with the Bible's warning against "the deceitfulness of riches" (Matt. 13:22). Not only wealth, but also God's gifts of life, time, abilities, and skills are blessings to sustain us in our calling. These gifts are given us to share the Gospel of Jesus Christ throughout the world and to support the needy. They become a curse when abused for our own selfish purposes.

It is simplistic to say that the rich should give all their wealth away or that the Bible shows that wealth is bad. God Himself is the Donor of riches. Christ's lesson teaches that it is a lack of love, not an abundance of money, that harms a person.

Let us also recognize that wealth may come in many forms. There are also great gifts of talent, beauty, and love—special gifts that money cannot buy. Any of these gifts can become a god.

Servants Seek the Lord First

In Matt. 6:33 Jesus gives the key or the main principle for our security and happiness in life, when He says: "Seek first the kingdom of God and His righteousness, and all these things shall be added to you." Everyone on earth is looking for security and happiness, most of them in possessions and things. We will find true happiness only as we heed Jesus' advice: Seek the Lord first.

In order to help us understand this lesson, Jesus teaches a series of lessons in Matt. 6:19–33. The first lesson is in vv. 19–21: We are not to lay up treasures for ourselves on earth, "where moth and rust destroy and where thieves break in and steal," but lay up treasures in heaven, where they are safe. He says: "Where your treasure is, there your heart will be also." Don't hold on to things for security and happiness. If a prized possession becomes useless or is taken away, where will security and happiness be? Our treasure is Christ, so no matter whether we have much or little, we are secure. If our treasure is possessions, then our heart will soon be unhappy. Our treasure is that in which we take great delight and toward which we devote our greatest efforts.

How much do we store up here on earth and how much in heaven? How much is enough? Without realizing it, we redefine *enough* again and again to accommodate our greed. We must decide how much saving we should do in the name of responsibility and exactly where the line is drawn between prudence and greed.

Vv 22–23 tell that the eye is the lamp of the body and that the body's light or darkness will depend on how strong or weak the eye is. Looking at the context of Matt. 6, we wonder how this fits into all that Jesus is teaching. It appears that this refers to the eyes of faith. Let us read the verses as we insert the words "of faith" after "eye" or "light": The lamp of the body is the eye of faith. If therefore your eye of faith is good, your whole body will be full of light. But if your eye of faith is bad, your whole body will be full of darkness. If therefore the light of faith that is in you is darkness, how great is that darkness!

The truth of this can be seen in people who destroy themselves although they have the best things that life has to offer, such as wealth, honor, position, power, and great beauty. Why do they want to end it all? Because without faith they are in darkness. Life makes no sense to them; indeed, it is nonsense. They are not really happy despite their superior earthly advantages. In this context a sound eye seems to mean having a right perspective. So long as we are torn between material things and heavenly things, our judgment will be clouded and we will not be capable of "seeing" matters as God sees them. Our view of life will determine our goals in life. The lesson: Faith is the greatest factor of life.

V. 24 shows us that we cannot serve two masters, God and possessions. It is impossible to devote our hearts and allegiance equally to God and to possessions, for we were created to have one Center, God. To try to have two centers creates misery, so that we cannot enjoy either spiritual things or material ones. We are doomed to dissatisfaction. The choice is between slavery to created things or the freedom of serving the Creator. The more time we devote to God in worship, studying His Word, and serving Him, the less time we will have available for what is of little value. Keep the focus on God, not on material things.

V. 25 tells us that we should not worry about what we will eat or how we will be clothed, for life is more important than food, and the body more than clothing. We should not put material things first, asking, "A man has to live, doesn't he?" Does a person have to live outside the will of God? Does a person have to take things into his own hands and deny the providence of God? When Jesus asks, "Is not life more than food and the body more than clothing?" He is stressing priorities. We are to leave the providing to Him. To say it another way, we are to make proper choices in our daily lives but are to stay out of the "God business" of providing as He has promised. Feeding and clothing us is His chief concern, not ours.

V. 26 gives us assurance that God will provide our food as He does for the birds, who don't worry about it. Have you ever seen a bird with wrinkled beak and anxious eyes, sitting and wondering where his food will come from? Will God not feed us, since we are of greater value than the birds?

V. 27 informs us that worry will not add anything to our span of life or our stature. Taking matters into our own hand by paying for groceries first will not guarantee one extra day of life. Nor will we live one day less by giving to God first. Anxiety assures nothing.

Vv. 28–30 find Jesus raising the basic issue about which He is really concerned: faith or the lack of it. It is a lack of faith that makes us choose earthly rather than heavenly treasure. God provides for the plants, as He also cares for animals, fish, and birds. Certainly He will care for His special creation, man. Faith will not cling to material things, but to the Giver. The focal point of life is faith. *Christ,* not things, is our happiness and security.

V. 31 is a repetition of v. 25 in the questions, "What shall we eat, drink, or wear?" We should not worry and ask that. Jesus is indicating what our priorities are to be.

V. 32 provides two reasons why we should not put possessions before God: (1) The heathen seek after those things, and we are not unbelievers; (2) God made us and knows what we need, and He will provide. Pagans have no higher good or goal than food, cars, home, things; so anxiety and worry are appropriate for them. Not for the Christian. In a sense, Jesus is saying, "Do you think God forgot about you? Let Him play His role as the heavenly Father, the Provider." The doctrine of preservation is involved.

V. 33, "Seek God first and you will have your food, drink, and clothes," is the key principle for security and happiness in life. This is the answer to the question, "Who comes first?" At this point the questions of vv. 25 and 31 become urgent, for a person might cry out: "God gave me this family, so doesn't He want me to feed and clothe them?" Yes, but not as a priority before God. He tells us to seek first the greater value of heavenly treasure, and points out the folly of seeking food, clothes, cars, and homes before we are right with Him and doing the works of the Kingdom. V. 33 is the New Testament principle of living.

The lesson here is not to worry, because God will take care of you. But the real point is to seek God first, and you have nothing to worry about. There is no need to be anxious, because God promises to supply food and clothes. "All these things" are necessities rather than optional things of life. Luther stresses this great promise as he recognizes that some people have a very uncomfortable situation; but God knows all about it. Luther writes, "God will not let your situation make a liar out of Him. Just believe!"

Put God first in everything and at all times. God will keep His promise to give us the necessities of life.

Life-Style Gift

The truly motivated Christian steward will want to make a

commitment of all his resources, to be shared with our Savior by the Biblical principle of firstfruits and generous percentage giving, as God gives faith and grace. Beyond such practice of Biblical principles, each Christian steward may be challenged to provide an extra gift for a special cause, using what is not absolutely needed. Most of us have adopted a higher life-style than is required for true productivity and joy in life.

This special life-style gift is based on Christ's parable of the talents (Matt. 25:14–30), in which Jesus has told us that God, the Owner of all, expects dividends and interest from what He gives His creatures. He condemned the man who buried his talent and gained nothing from what he had, and He commended those who gained interest on their investments. We have some possessions which are not really useful to us and which could help in God's work.

Let us prayerfully consider the gift of some possession which we really do not need. It may be something which we have purchased or inherited, something of small or great value, but a possession which earns no interest in our hands and would provide great eternal dividends in God's hands.

Think of something which is in a closet or attic, in a box or out in the open, which is presently useless to Christ's kingdom. It is not necessary for our livelihood or pleasure, and would produce much good for the work of our church. That possession may be jewelry, some equipment for which we no longer have use, some fairly expensive knickknack or antique, a stamp or other collection. Whatever it may be, consider selling it and giving all or a good percentage of the income to a special cause in the Lord's kingdom.

How to sell it? Take it to a flea market, or work together with other members of your congregation through a parking lot or garage sale. Advertise your articles in the newspapers. Do it as individual Christians, not in the name of the church. Ask God's blessing that there may be a good market for your gifts and that a good payment be received for the sake of His work.

It is possible that considerable profit could be made from otherwise useless articles by following this approach. Personal joy will be enlarged as the value of those possessions will be multiplied many times through use in the kingdom of our Lord Jesus Christ.

The Servant's Concern for the Poor and Underprivileged

Jesus' ministry demonstrated concern for the poor and needy. His primary mission was to die for the sins of men, but He also showed God's mercy and compassion by feeding the 5,000, healing the sick, and caring for the poor. His entire ministry was a life dedicated to serving the needs of people. Peter said that Jesus "went about doing good and healing all who were oppressed by the devil, for God was with Him" (Acts 10:38).

We are to "do good to all, especially to those who are of the household of faith" (Gal. 6:10). Heb. 13:2–3 reminds us that we are to show hospitality to strangers and to remember those who are ill-treated or in prison. John warns that if we close our hearts against a needy brother, the love of God does not abide in us (1 John 3:17).

The storehouse of heaven is open to meet all these needs. God gives His supplies in two ways: directly and indirectly. To accomplish His design, God offers His supply house. All of God's gifts are a divine investment upon which the Investor expects full return for the church, for oneself, and for the good of others.

Jesus' teachings show that He wants to be sought, found, and served through the poor. His description of the Last Judgment equates gifts made to the poor as made to Him: "Truly, I say to you, as you did it to one of the least of these My brethren, you did it to Me" (Matt. 25:40 RSV). We serve Him through them. It is the Lord's will to provide opportunity for the servant of Christ to display love in deed. God keeps jealous watch over treatment of the poor (Is. 3:14–15). It was Sodom's fatal crime that she neglected the poor and exploited those who were weak (Ezek. 16:49). When the rich man Dives had opportunity at his doorstep to show love for the poor man, he failed the test and went to hell. God could not portray more graphically the importance of Christian love for the poor. Our materialism tempts us to misunderstand Biblical truths related to the poor. It is as difficult for those not in want to acknowledge that all their possessions are God's gifts as it is for those who are in want to recognize that their want is an opportunity for God to provide for them through others. The latter long for riches, and the former are determined to hoard them.

Social reformers do not hesitate to use the poor as a lever upon the public conscience. The theology of liberation (a revolutionary approach) not only confuses this matter but is not a proper response to the Biblical injunction or to the abuse of wealth. Both misuse the Word for their own designs. Vital to God's servant is proclamation, not revolution. We are not dealing with limited resources, but with God's supply house.

Often the aim of social reformers is to exercise power in redistribution of money and property (taking from some and giving to others by law or government order) rather than production and gaining more dividends to share. Profit is the interest which God requires in the parable of the talents, but social reformers condemn it. The church, not the government, is designed to be the powerful force for feeding the hungry.

Redistribution of property and income by force spoils production, and reformers frequently find that there is less and less to redistribute. This is dismantling God-given resources and daring anyone to be faithful with them or to enlarge them; people will work less, save less, invest less, produce less. It is making man's supply house the all-in-all. It is unbelief about God's supply house.

It must be said here that the reason why government gets into the "giving to the poor" business is because Christians and the church have failed to be faithful to their God-given responsibilities. God's supply house is sufficient for Christians everywhere to feed all of the poor of the world. Neighbors should care for neighbors and others in the community. The Bible tells of distant Christians who gave offerings to help the poor in Jerusalem. That's God's plan. Today, too, there are many obvious situations that call for such giving by Christians to the hungry throughout the world. The problem is sin, not possessions. The omission of Christian charity is one of Christians failing to give as God intended. Spiritual reality is evidenced by physical involvement.

David Chilton in his book *Productive Christians in an Age of Guilt Manipulators,*[3] shows how social reformers are rewriting the Scriptures and defying God's plan that we all become enriched from His storehouse.

John Perkins, another Christian writer, proposes regeneration, production, and sharing, observes how government welfare systems have failed, and says that Christians must see the oppressed and poor as a Macedonian call.

Aside from the denial of the Biblical injunction to Christians, the redistribution policy destroys incentive among the poor to help themselves and hurts human dignity. Such handouts create demands for more handouts. People come to feel that the government (the giver of gifts) owes them a living, while they're ignorant of God's storehouse, from which Christians should be giving. Christians and churches have the resources to do the job. If anyone doubts it, the two fishes and five loaves (God's supply house) are just a starting point.

In the Old Testament all families were required to have personal contact with the poor in their communities, insuring that funds for the poor would be given to those who were truly in need. God's law was gracious to the poor: He commended charity toward them and made various provisions, such as gleaning, on their behalf. However, the poor did not have an unqualified claim on the goodness of others. God's law sought to teach responsibility both to those who had and those who did not have.

We can choose between two methods of social change: regeneration or revolution; production or confiscation. The Bible teaches regeneration and production as the way. It is a wrong supposition, by the way, that the riches of some are the cause of the poverty of others.

Social reform such as socialism cannot produce wealth, but only destroy it; it can only confiscate. On the other hand, God's store house brings physical and material blessings to a culture. God commands that Christians work, be content, give, and pray. That is the way God will meet the needs of the hungry.

Slaves of materialism, whether rich or poor, need liberty, but they cannot be legislated into it. If they are not bound to Christ, no matter what a government does, they will still be slaves and all will be in trouble. The real issue is faithful obedience to the will of God. Governments cannot produce regeneration; only God can do so. Governments cannot effectively and adequately feed the poor; only Christian servants can.

Churches should consider being resource centers for gifts to the poor by food and clothing banks to meet legitimate needs. Various churches and agencies already have resource centers that offer supplies in the name of Jesus.

The Servant's Giving for Larger Church Needs

The Christian servant embraces supply-side stewardship, for God supplies and multiplies the seed He sows and increases the fruits of the steward's righteousness, while the latter is "enriched in everything for all liberality" (2 Cor. 9:10–11). The steward will be rich toward God (8:5), toward others (8:16; 9:12), and toward the church's mission (9:1–2).

When you sow or invest in God's kingdom, you will prosper spiritually, confess the Gospel, provide for those in need, cause many to give thanks for your sowing, and give glory to God. That's a great harvest. The more seed planted, the more harvested. The only limitations are the ones that we create by our lack of faith and lack of sowing.

In view of the haphazard giving, the "makeup" campaigns, and the capital fund drives, we ask the question: Can the church's local and worldwide mission be maintained solely through planned, firstfruit, generous, proportionate giving, together with appropriate praise offerings? Or are we stuck with no other alternative than regular big collections from churches which average about 2-1/2% of personal income given to God? Are the church's perceived and stated needs the measure of giving for the members?

The principles of giving in both Testaments reveal that all members were taught the Biblical principles of tithing and/or planned, firstfruit, proportionate giving. When larger gifts were requested, these were for special needs which were not met by givers who were already generous. They were not gifts to meet basic mission obligations which the church had failed to meet because the majority of members were giving leftovers. Their main funding did not depend upon capital but rather upon income as it was earned.

There are various situations where some are giving only 1%, 2%, or 3% of their personal income to the Lord while their special gift for a five-year period may amount to only an additional 1%, 2%, or 3%. They often believe that they are doing an extraordinary thing, which they are not. On the basis of New Testament grace principles, their giving cannot be pleasing to God. Big offerings based on institutional needs without reference to proportionate giving are a maintenance and survival stewardship approach of fund raising which will create increased pressure upon the church and agencies to perform aggressively.

What is the problem when churches major in marketing and sociological principles to raise large amounts of money? The wisdom of the world is confused with the wisdom of God. Often Law and Gospel motivation are mixed. Moralizing is cloaked in Gospel terminology. Pressure, which sometimes is offensive, is placed on some members to produce.

Definitions of good contributions are usually inadequate, for from man's viewpoint Ananias and Sapphira gave a good offering, while the widow's mite would be disqualified in the Big Drive. Some of the sociological fund-raising principles set aside the liberty of givers, as their small gift is refused during the "Large Gift Campaign." Their small gift may be as big as the widow's mite—a far bigger percentage than the large gifts of the rich.

Various techniques are to be questioned. A variety of sales techniques appeal to the pride of the natural man so that he will be moved to action. He is given the hint that he should not ride out this successful effort. Success is equated with man-made principles and goals. To guarantee success big fund-raising drives employ sociological policies, analyze statistics, and graph individual responses. On the basis of these standards, projected results are calculated, and the methodology and messages are proposed. Thus we may be told that one dollar given by the "big" givers will generate seven dollars from all the others. Biblically speaking, human appeals only generate human actions, not divine power to give fully from God's supply house.

Various church bodies and congregations have claimed success when large sums of money were raised. Too often they do not seem to notice the failure to gain gifts from a large percentage of the people. Sometimes as high as 60% to 70% do not give. When only a minority participate and spiritual growth is minimal, success is questionable.

It is true that quite often people contribute to a cause in direct relationship to the manner in which they are asked. But when we teach them Biblical principles, they give much more year by year, not just sporadically when they are asked. The asking of specific sums is important for the unregenerate man, for he finds such logic and organization appealing to him. He enjoys knowing that he is an important part of a campaign.

Unregenerate man will also participate as he is inspired by a knowledge of how the program is progressing and whether it will be successful. Such techniques are the way of the Law, which undermines the Scriptural principles of giving. There is the need of the member to give and to make a commitment, but that is to be gained by a message of grace, not the compulsion of needs.

Does the Christian servant really require a "needs presentation" in order to respond to a program which should have been handled by the ongoing firstfruit gifts of the people year by year?

Churches need to shy away from behavioristic methods which tell us that people give better when they know they are giving to extraordinary needs, that success is assured when they know what they are to give in a campaign, and when they are asked in a specific manner.

What is the practical and reasonable thing to do that is also Biblical? Educate every member in Biblical principles of giving. Then challenge them to increase giving by at least 1% of personal income for the special offering. Firstfruit, proportionate givers to not lapse or go back to their old ways, so this increase would be produced also the second year, the third year. This is true of those who have been practicing it and those who are new at it. We title this approach "Plus 1." This means to increase our giving by at least 1% of our income until our faith is stretched to the point where we must increase more slowly.

Plus 1

The following is the message we propose to be shared with the members as they are visited for a special gift:

If the earth and all therein is the Lord's, then the question is not how much of mine do I have to give to God. The question is, "How much of God's money will I keep?" All we have—100%— is sacred to God.

Giving money to God does not come naturally. It appears more natural to complain that God wants our gifts of financial resources. God's people in the Old Testament (Israel) sometimes grumbled about offering: "In every place incense shall be offered to My name, and a pure offering; for My name shall be great among the nations. . . . But you profane it . . ." (Mal. 1:11–12). Three facts face us: Our possessions are God's, not ours; God wants generous offerings given joyfully; He detests complainers and poor givers.

What does God want? He wants us to give *from* what He has given us, not *to* church needs. God asks more of us than merely meeting church budgets, most of which can be met while people are giving an average of 2 1/2% of their incomes to God—leftovers!

God has outlined His plan for our giving habits in the Word, where His total will for our lives is revealed. That *plan* includes:

1. Give to God *first,* before buying groceries, clothes, car, and home. Jesus: "Seek first the kingdom of God and His righteousness, and all these things [food, drink, clothes], shall be added to you" (Matt. 6:33).

2. Give a planned percentage or portion of your income to Christ's church, as seen in 1 Cor. 16:2. Both Old and New Testaments emphasize a portion or part set aside for God's work—sacred or separated for Kingdom tasks.

3. Give a generous part or percent to God. As New Testament believers we will prayerfully consider whether we will give more or less than God's people in the Old Testament—10 cents out of each dollar. To give a small portion is contrary to the new nature in Christ. To give a generous part, 10 percent *and more,* is a true expression of the "Christ in us." Tithing in itself is an inadequate expression of faith. God requires more of us than 10% of our income. Grace disallows the use of the tithe to condemn and threaten rather than guide and encourage.

4. *Faith* sets the percentage set apart for Christ's kingdom. God tells us: "It is required in stewards that one be found faithful" (1 Cor. 4:2)—full of faith. The weaker the faith, the lower the percentage. The stronger the faith, the higher the percentage. God does not give us a law under grace as to what exact percentage will please Him. Growing faith will be expressed in a growing percentage.

Some are giving three cents or less of every dollar of income. Others are giving five or seven cents, and some 10 and 15 cents of every dollar. Whatever portion or percentage, we will ask ourselves whether this part is the true measure of our faith and love. As we grow in faith, we will give a larger portion. We need to pray, "Lord, increase my faith."

5. Generous percentage giving is a *grace* from God. Paul said:

"We make known to you the grace [gift] of God bestowed on the churches of Macedonia: that . . . their deep poverty abounded in the riches of their liberality" (2 Cor. 8:1–2). Generous proportionate giving is a gift (grace) from God for which each of us should pray. Christ's love compels us to give that way. What is your response by God's grace?

Since Christ's love compels us to grow in giving, we will want to increase the percentage we give to God. If you are giving less than 10% to the Lord at this time, will you ask God for the grace (gift) and strength of faith to increase it by at least 1%, 2%, 3%, or 4% of your personal income? That means that if you are giving 3%, and increase by 3%, you would be giving firstfruits of 6% in the future. Pray God for strength to increase your giving by at least 1% of your personal income. If that seems very difficult, wrestle with God in prayer and ask the Holy Spirit for strength and that gift or grace. If you are above 10% in giving, then possibly you will want to ask God for the gift of increasing your giving by 1% of your personal income to provide for the special ministries of your church. Everyone is challenged to set aside at least 1% for that important world mission cause.

Will you take a close look at what you are giving and make a step of growth by going through this exercise?

a. My estimated annual income is. . . . . $ ___________
b. A tithe (10%) of this would be . . . . $ ___________
c. My present weekly offerings are . . . . $ ___________
d. This amounts to an annual percentage of $ ___________
e. I will increase my giving by 1%, 2%, 3%, 4% (circle one) of my personal income
f. I plan my percentage offering for next year to amount to . . . . $ ___________
g. This will represent a weekly offering of about . . . . $ ___________
h. Of this offering I will give to the Special Offering the amount of . . . . $ ___________

May God give you a strong faith to adopt priorities pleasing to Him so that more workers may be trained for God's kingdom and more effective ministries may be conducted for the sake of the Gospel of Jesus Christ.

MY COMMITMENT

As I am alive in Christ by God's grace through Jesus, the Author and Finisher of my faith, I renew my commitment to live only for Him by the power of the Holy Spirit. Understanding the need to grow in grace and knowledge by the compelling love of Christ, I will seek to get rid of hindrances to faithful use of my abilities, time, and money for God's work. I will seek to live for Christ more closely and to grow in my personal giving (mark one of the following):

______ I give 10% or more to God and will increase my giving 1% (or more) of my personal income.

______ My gifts to God amount to less than 10%, and I'll increase by 1%, 2%, 3%, 4%, or ____ % of my personal income (circle one).

______ I will begin firstfruit proportionate giving, sharing a percentage of my personal income which represents a growing faith and which will glorify Christ and help advance His kingdom.

Being committed to provide for the ministries of my congregation and church body, I will give to the special ministries involved in the Special Offering:

A large gift in the amount of $ ________________ .

A "life-style" gift of ________________________ .

A special offering for the next three years which totals $ ________________ .

As God's way of firstfruit proportionate giving is to be adopted by individuals, so the congregation should adopt priorities for mission outreach in its state or province, country, and world. As members of a church, we will encourage our congregation to share a growing portion of all gifts for sending more workers and missionaries everywhere.

As the *Plus 1* concept and principle is incorporated into visits to prospective donors for Big Offerings, congregations will benefit by a strong Biblical message to their members. This will result in a permanent habit of firstfruit proportionate giving with a growing percentage to Kingdom-wide ministries. God is full of resources, which are best tapped by utilizing Biblical supply-side methods rather than maintenance-needs approaches.

CHAPTER FIVE

ABUNDANT SUPPLY OF INFORMATION—THE EDUCATION PROCESS

Great stewardship is the product of great communication which conveys God's great grace. What is produced is the result of stewardship education (or the lack of it). People are as they are fed and led. The principle of sowing and reaping comes into sharp focus in education. Jesus did not say, "Go, collect money!" but "Go, teach, make disciples!"

Maintenance and exhortation approaches with little sound Biblical education result in perpetual crisis management and a deadly drift from program to program, meeting to meeting, crisis to crisis, without strong purpose and direction.

An educational process which provides a generous supply of God's Word will be the seed that grows to bountiful fruit in the lives of individual Christians. Spiritual growth results from tapping the total supply of the Word and trusting God's promises. Fruit is dependent on Biblical principles, not forms, methods, and programs, which may vary greatly.

There is a need to provide adequate information before a commitment is made. People give as they know and believe, not as they are able. People may say that they will give as they are able, but who truly knows his own ability even with the use of a computer? We give as we know and believe. It is the leader's responsibility to provide knowledge, and the Holy Spirit's task to give belief and faith, which He provides through a generous supply of God's Word. Many people are starving from a lack of the Word.

We need to use the same energy on the educational process as on maintenance programs and special campaigns for financial survival. This means the end of marshaling our members to work in special fund-raising and crisis programs. They are challenged to utilize the same energy in basic educational programs with objectives of deepened understanding, new spiritual growth, and stronger commitment to spiritual renewal. Ezek. 36 reveals that renewal is for God's sake, for the world's sake, and for our sake: ". . . for My holy name's sake . . . and the nations shall know that I am the Lord. . . . For I will . . . bring you into your own land" (vv. 22–24). All of this is by the Holy Spirit's power: "Then I will sprinkle clean water on you, and you shall be clean; I will cleanse you from your filthiness and from all your idols. . . . I will put My Spirit within you and cause you to walk in My statutes" (vv. 25, 27).

Charlie Shedd's educational principle is a good approach for our stewardship efforts: "Study—the—Scriptures—and—see—what—God—says—to—you . . . Start—somewhere—and—develop—as—the—Lord—leads" plan. Never get between the people and God with human proposals, but always face them with God's Word. Come to a common agreement on the meaning of the Biblical texts dealing with stewardship, so that all are aware that God is speaking to them, *not* church leaders making a church proposal. Agree on the request and proposal that God makes. Then encourage members to be obedient to God's will, starting somewhere and growing in stewardship acts as the Holy Spirit empowers. This approach is to be practiced without exception in the educational process and individual programs.

The entire educational and edification process requires that all communication be Biblical, with doctrinal content, also in application and methodological considerations. Therefore leaders and teachers must know the Scriptures well and be sufficiently mature to communicate that Word effectively.

Every adult must be a student of the Bible. One of the chief goals is to get every member into the habit of Bible study. There is a direct relation between spiritual strength or growth and the amount and quality of Christian education and Bible study. All adults are expected to be growing in and through the Word. A growth-restricting obstacle is the "confirmation/graduation syndrome" of many churches. This is one of the greatest hindrances to getting people into Bible study.

Education in the church is a means to an end, not an end in itself. The end is growth in knowledge, faith, and love expressed fully in daily life.

Necessary Ingredients or Components

Sixteen ingredients or components are part of the comprehensive activities involved in an effective educational process. These need to be understood and integrated into the different methodologies utilized for organizing the Lord's mission in our congregation.

Ingredient or Component	Descriptive Phrase
1. Prayer	Ask and expect God to do the miraculous
2. Worship	Experience meaningful corporate celebration
3. Education	Involve a maximum number of members in relevant Bible study
4. Purpose	Unite around common objectives
5. Diagnosis	Analyze the local church and the community
6. Priorities	Emphasize most important activities and values
7. Planning Process	Project ways to achieve objectives
8. Programming	Build ministries which move toward objectives

9. Climate	Radiate love, service, witness, and expectancy
10. Leadership	Motivate and guide toward objectives
11. Spiritual Gifts	Discover and utilize the gifts of all members
12. Absorption	Establish a strong sense of belonging
13. Small Groups	Develop deep interpersonal relationships
14. Discipleship	Teach for commitment and spiritual multiplication
15. Intensive Training	Equip with knowledge, skills, and character for leadership
16. Evangelism	Present the Gospel effectively

Important Educational Principle

A key principle for education and commitment involves the reaching of the heart, mind, will, and spirit in preparation, proclamation, persuasion, and participation. Our educational process incorporates these educational principles. The focus and its adversary to good learning and good stewardship are our concern for these four areas:

PREPARATION (Heart)—Relationship

Focus: Open Mind Toward Servanthood
Adversary: Pride, Independence, Apathy

PREPARATION (Mind)—Revelation

Focus: Communication of the Word
Adversary: Ignorance, Complacency, Earthly Distractions, Self-Centeredness

PERSUASION (Will)—Response

Focus: Commitment to Biblical Terms for Spiritual Growth
Adversary: Procrastination, Indecision, Double-Mindedness, Pull of the World

PARTICIPATION (Spirit)—Action

Focus: Function as a Member of the Body of Christ
Adversary: Individualism, Isolation, Indifference

The Educational Program for Stewardship

If there is to be sufficient intake for generous stewardship output, a complete educational program will be required every year. Now we outline the approach required for preparing the stewards for a proper stewardship commitment. We will be sowing the seed inadequately if we cut short the educational contacts necessary for a bountiful harvest.

As you read these paragraphs, you may question the necessity of such a comprehensive plan of education. Please keep in mind the Biblical principle by the Holy Spirit, "Sow a little, reap a little; sow a lot, reap a lot." We have discovered that those who have faithfully sown the seed of God's Word in the nine-week educational program have seen a drastic change of understanding, attitude, and action on the part of Christian stewards.

1. Six weeks of sermons and Bible studies on a special theme.

Through experience and field testing we have learned the importance of using a concentrated period of time to build understanding and interest. Six Sundays are scheduled for this conditioning phase, at which time sermons, Bible studies, lay talks, and children's object lessons are presented. This is an important preparation time to condition the members to meditate on six vital aspects of a specific stewardship theme. Seven of the Stewardship Growth Series and Guidebooks have already been published, offering suggested sermon outlines, Bible study outlines, lay talks, and children's object lessons on the themes: "Lord, Let It Happen to Me as You Said!" "I Am Ready to Live," "Living for Christ," "Christian Stewards Using God's Gifts," "Called Together for Blessing," "God's Supply—Our Trust," and "New Steps of Faith." Each of these has been utilized in churches in order to sow the seed bountifully.

During these six weeks church leaders plan for enlarged worship attendance and Bible class attendance. People are encouraged to accept a short-term challenge to worship and study together for those weeks.

The elders or deacons, together with all active worshipers, fervently promote church attendance among the inactive and delinquents.

The Education Committee, together with those members

who attend Bible class regularly, organizes a Bible study attendance effort with the goal that there should be a major percentage increase of members attending Bible class during these six weeks. It is vital that during these six weeks one or two new Bible classes be organized in small congregations, and more than two new classes in larger congregations. Conducting more classes with new teachers will provide additional opportunities for members to attend and will impress the members with the fact that you mean business. Your experience should be that at least half of the new attendees, having broken their nonattendance habits, will continue to attend in the permanent classes. These short-term opportunities and goals are vital both for breaking poor Bible study habits and for gaining new interest in Bible study. Thus this effort increases Bible knowledge and increases attendance too.

2. Reach every member with a Bible Study Booklet.

Most important is the controlled presentation of a Bible study printed in a booklet, spending up to two hours with each member in presentation and discussion. Each of the above seven series offers a Bible Study Booklet on the theme, and each is a summary of the six topics for the six weeks.

The first impression of some leaders about these Bible Study Booklets is that they are too lengthy and people will not sit that long. Wrong! Experience has shown that less time means considerably less understanding and commitment—"Sow a little, reap a little." These booklets are to be studied with every member of the congregation, including inactives and delinquents.

Recently, leaders of several California congregations informed us about their experience especially through this Bible study approach with delinquents. One found three of those families now worshiping regularly. Another found four delinquent families worshiping regularly, with one attending Bible class weekly.

"Come to church" invitations to delinquents and inactives are totally inadequate. An emphasis on worship alone is totally inadequate. What is needed is active worship and well-planned Bible study through which the Word instructs and activates by the Holy Spirit. This will result in a new understanding of, and a new interest in, the relationship with Jesus Christ and commitment to Him. Remember, "Sow a lot, reap a lot." God promises that His Word will not return void, and so it should be expected that a certain number of people will respond positively.

Where to use the booklet? Members can be reached through a series of group meetings at the church, in "cottage meetings" in homes, in personal interviews scheduled at the church, or in every member visits. In each case all absentees or people who have not been contacted should be visited. There can be no exception. One of the big failures of churches everywhere is that they reach only 40% and 60% of their members in stewardship education. That is why there are usually "two congregations": one which regularly hears the message through personal contacts and one which is never reached. It is time to stop this tragedy, for we are contributing to the delinquency of members by failing to reach them with Bible study.

How to use the Bible Study Booklet? It must be a controlled presentation, where the leader makes certain that every word is read by himself or by one of the participants. It is good to request participants to read especially the Scripture portions. The leader should make comments as necessary on various paragraphs and various ideas. There must be a five-minute discussion after each one of the six parts, and at least a ten-minute discussion at the end.

If two hours seems too long, then do not expect a big harvest out of little sowing. Remember, people give as they know and believe. We have the responsibility to share information and increase knowledge so that the Holy Spirit can strengthen faith.

What Do You Expect?

Do you want to stimulate vision and awareness of God's gift and cultivate members to be strong stewards of all that God has given? Are you looking for a meaningful way to handle stewardship problems and challenges? Do you desire to use an exciting Biblical way to overcome church pressures now and in future years? Do you wish to initiate healthy growth and massive change toward better management of abilities and possessions on the part of your members?

Do you want to apply truths, principles, messages, and methods of sanctification in a more effective manner through your church boards and committees? Do you want to disciple more leaders to be good examples and effective teachers in stewardship? Do you want to build a greater number of committed members and leaders?

Do you want to gain the majority of your members for Bible study? Do you want to double or triple your church income without talking money? Do you want to use a distinctly Scriptural educational model designed to challenge the faith of members? Do you want enlarged commitment for the explosive end of the 20th century?

If you answered "Yes!" to most or all of the preceding questions, you should seriously consider the educational process. Write your own, or you might consider the Stewardship Growth Series with the Guide Books and the Bible Study Booklets as a model.

Through such Bible study you are able to reach the wide spectrum of members, no matter where they are on the scale of spiritual understanding, attitudes, commitments, and life-styles. Paul reminds us in 1 Cor. 2 and 3 that there are four kinds of people spiritually: (1) natural man (without regeneration): "The natural man does not receive the things of the Spirit of God, for they are foolishness to him; nor can he know them, because they are spiritually discerned" (2:14); (2) infant believers or spiritual babies: ". . . babes in Christ. I fed you with milk and not with solid food; for until now you were not able to receive it" (3:1–2); (3) carnal Christians, where the Old Man is too much in control: "For you are still carnal. For where there are envy, strife, and divisions among you, are you not carnal and behaving like mere men? For when one says, 'I am of Paul,' and another, 'I am of Apollos,' are you not carnal?" (3:3–4); (4) spiritually mature believers: "But he who is spiritual judges all things, yet he himself is rightly judged by no one. . . . And I, brethren, could not speak to you as to spiritual people" (2:15, 3:1).

For some people, we will be satisfied to see growth in understanding in one year, others a change in attitude in one year, others a change in general commitment, and others a change in life-style. The church cannot program individuals and put them all in one category.

The educational and discipling approach is the solution to our problems. Jesus told us to teach. The grace approach demands patience and acceptance of God's timetable for the leaders and the members. Growth should not be forced by legalistic denunciations and exhortations.

The proposed educational model does not suggest new structures or programs outside the structures and activities that should already be present in the congregation. This educational process merely intensifies the preaching, teaching, and personal contacts that are inherent in God's plan for the congregation. The intensified program builds permanent participation in people who are sporadic and somewhat lax. Thus this educational approach helps the congregation meet one of its key objectives: getting more members to worship and study God's Word regularly.

Focus of the Educational Process

There are growth principles for this educational process which we need to embody. Ministry centers on the Great Commission, with a priority on exploring and employing spiritual gifts. All members, not just 40% to 60%, must be involved. There needs to be flexibility and mobility. The John 15 pruning process is to be practiced, as branches are to respond to pruning. We need to understand the culture within which we work, including the varied cultures among members. New ministries need to be developed.

The corporate body finds its center in Christ, who said: "I will build My church." We don't build the church, Christ does. He involves us in the edifying process as through the Spirit we are equipped to speak the Word to each other for building up each member and the entire Body. We are to develop a support system and meet the needs where people hurt. We understand where we are and where we need to go. There is a great expectancy, relying on the Holy Spirit for miraculous things.

The primary emphasis is on education for parents rather than children as the main targets of Christian growth. We will reach families, not just children. The church should help parents raise their children. Sunday schools and Christian day schools are the "boot camp" for young believers, where a spiritual building program is being undertaken.

Body growth is seen as important, as is spiritual growth. There will be a sound and solid Biblical curriculum so that people will be eager to come, for people go where they are fed.

Evangelism

Evangelism will be done in homes, backyards, places of work, and social occasions, not basically in worship services. Home Bible study is the model of evangelism. Plans and programs will saturate the community. Being obedient to Christ's parables, we will not just search, but keep on until we find.

Finances

Finances will focus on ministry rather than on maintenance, on God's supply rather than on survival. There will be an indigenous attitude of giving *from*, not *to*. There will be a commitment to digging and fertilizing, not fruit picking.

Facilities

Facilities will be functional, with a priority of multiple service over new construction. There will be house cell units for training members, and the facilities will be used effectively for equipping leaders.

Objectives and Goals

The chief Biblical objective is renewal of individual members and of the Body, a constant reformation. The Twelve Steps should be facilitated.[1] There should be great anticipation of the annual nine-week educational process of the Stewardship Growth Series and eager participation by members week after week.

A growing number of people will be eager to learn the truth, for Jesus promised: "You shall know the truth, and the truth shall make you free" (John 8:32). People with all kinds of addictions and enslavements will find freedom to become true servants of Christ and provide bountiful financial gifts to enlarge old ministries and to begin new ones. Although there will be regular problems and aberrations to be corrected by edifying through the Word, love for others will be a way of life.

Fear and depression, caused by wrong values, desires, and attitudes, will be solved by love which empowers us to quit habits of breaking God's spiritual and physical laws. "There is no fear in love; but perfect love casts out fear. . . . He who fears has not been made perfect in love" (1 John 4:18). That love whose source is God's supply of love will diminish fear and hopelessness. We are not born with that love. It must be given to us and developed by Supernatural Power.

Human beings are born incomplete, missing something. They need a vital missing element, which is the Spirit of God found in Jesus Christ. The fruit of that Spirit is love . . . kindness . . . faithfulness . . . self-control (Gal. 5:22–23).

God's purpose in regeneration is to develop a holy, righteous, and loving character. The aim is to love God with all our heart, soul, mind, and strength, and our neighbor as ourself (Mark 12:30–32). That love is not the way of hate, competition, lust, envy, jealousy, covetousness, selfishness, or exalting oneself over others. As we tap God's spiritual power, He will intervene in our lives to replace these things with love. He promises: "I dwell . . . with him who has a contrite and humble spirit . . . to revive the heart of the contrite ones (Is. 57:15). The growth process is summed up in 2 Tim. 1:5–7: "God has not given us a spirit of fear, but of power and of love and of a sound mind."

There will undoubtedly be broad acceptance of the objectives outlined in this section. The problem lies in their implementation in the daily affairs of the church. It happens regularly when a pastor or leader proposes some activity which is part of the educational process and which grows out of these Biblical objectives that the first question asked is, "How much will it cost?" Such a maintenance attitude is also revealed by spending much time in church meetings with techniques, fund-raising proposals, and how the budget can be cut. At that time grace and supply-side objectives are negated by the tyranny of the urgent and of survival.

The first and main objective is that God's Word should be taught effectively so that by the Holy Spirit's power every member of every congregation may confess Jesus Christ not only as Savior but as Lord, and "live under Him in His kingdom and serve Him." This means obedience to the Great Commission of Jesus Christ.

The basic objectives are found in the Scriptures: "That the man of God may be complete, thoroughly equipped for every good work" (2 Tim. 3:17), and also to make him "complete in every good work to do His will, working in you what is well pleasing in His sight, through Jesus Christ, to whom be glory forever and ever. Amen" (Heb. 13:21).

The basic purpose is to gain adequate responses from all members, built on the fact that God has given them all the resources needed to evangelize and missionize effectively as World Christians. This education is to enrich their relationship with God and their fellowmen and to add quality to their spiritual lives. All are to hold Christ as the main priority in their lives, committing their abilities and money in proportion to the gifts that God has given them.

With renewal in mind, here are *other objectives:*

Replace the "maintenance" model of church work with a creative mission outreach and educational process.

Gain every member as a Bible student, seeking to be obedient to the Great Commission, as understanding, attitudes, and habits become aligned with the will of God.

Change the focus from giving to church needs and budgets *toward a focus on* individual giving of all that God has given, a focus away from the institution toward individual expression of faith.

Instead of requesting volunteers to fill church tasks and positions, teach each believer to recognize and utilize God-given abilities and spiritual gifts in the church.

Replace giving which centers on doing one's share in meeting budgets and quotas with planned, firstfruit, generous, proportionate giving performed by the grace of God.

Strengthen the effectiveness of the total church program—stewardship, education, evangelism, edifying, fellowship, social welfare, and other Gospel tasks.

Broaden the base of leadership and gain more workers.

Initiate a commitment program for youth and teens.

Lift the vision of the congregation toward enlarged offerings for local work and for world missions.

Assure a strong stewardship committee to provide leadership to meet all stewardship challenges of the future.

The Christian steward is a person who is entrusted with a life redeemed by Christ. To be a steward is to follow where God leads by the abilities and strength He gives. Christian stewardship is the expression of the Christian faith. A steward is a servant-manager of all God's resources placed in his hands for use in his own life and in the church.

Evaluate Methods

There is nothing inherently wrong or sinful about an organization or system. As we know, organization and method are indispensable. Greed, pride, and envy do not come from a system; they are put into the system and change it toward the bad. Good things need to be put into the organization and methodology. To blame organizations and methods for the failures of people confuses cause and effect. Programs don't succeed or fail— people do. It isn't the program that works, people work.

Many of our arguments about methods are futile because we have not distinguished method as performance from method as principle or content conveyed through methods. Different methods produce great differences both in quantity and quality in the spiritual formation of the Christian community, its leadership and its discipling. Methods are important vehicles, but by themselves human methods do not strengthen churches.

As an example, modern equipment that is working perfectly is no guarantee that there will be a good crop. The seed and fertilizer are the vital factors. We cannot have an effective stewardship process without utilizing some means and methods, but that does not imply standardized techniques and tools.

North America is a method-oriented culture. We have a preoccupation to find the most efficient method, often resulting in a loss of the objectives and ends for which the means are employed. The Christian community is not immune to this "method mania." Christianity does not offer a "spiritual technology" which will provide wholeness and prosperity, or deliver the Holy Spirit, if we follow a set of prescribed disciplines.

In a pragmatic world it is difficult to argue against results, and especially hard to meet the competition when everyone is crying out for a better method, not a better product. Those who innovate a new and successful methodology invariably are the heroes.

Methods are human creations and should be oriented toward objectives and goals. The understanding and communicating of factors in a situation must be settled before we decide on a method. We dare not use methods that change the nature of the Gospel. The only force to make faithful and strong stewards is the force of Christ's love. How many of the "Hidden Persuaders" (Vance Packard, 1951) can be incorporated without turning proclamation into manipulation by method? Sometimes leaders select a method and insist that the rest of us fall in line, trying to legislate others.

Methods and strategies are invariably dynamic and time-bound. The ultimate strategy should always involve the formation of an educational process, for that is the essence of Christ's training and discipling approach. This means that we should continually discuss the assumptions upon which our strategies are based. These assumptions are difficult to set down correctly because they are assumptions about ourselves. This means that when we want stewardship change in people, there first must be a change in the stewardship leader. That's where method starts.

We are interested in renewal and discovery of what God's will is and what He wants accomplished by us. We should act responsibly and with integrity even when we are not sure what to do or what the exact results will be. But we cannot justify sloppy methods, lazy habits, and inexcusable actions that have little regard for an authentic message and the anticipated consequences. It is irresponsible to try to justify failure due to poor strategy or inadequate attitudes toward the body of Christ. God expects us as stewards to decide by faith what we are to be and do, and what we believe the outcomes of our lives and actions ought to be.

Educational methods require time and effort, but that is part of the growth process. That is why shortcuts like letter writing campaigns without every member contacts do little to deepen understanding of Biblical principles. Letters are good only if they are added to personal contacts. Failure to recruit sufficient workers for a stewardship educational program is a poor excuse for resorting to fund-raising drives by letters only. Anything less than a full training program for leaders and educational contacts with all members is submission to the maintenance mediocrity of fund-raising drives and campaigns.

Faithfulness is more than simply spending time and working hard at commendable stewardship activities. Faithfulness, not achievements, is the standard by which we will be judged. It is a matter of being faithful to God's requirements and of accomplishing His tasks. What counted in the parable of the talents was not good intentions, but the dividends derived from the resources received.

Stewardship leaders can easily forget that our sinful nature generates an unconscious drive to construct systems which too quickly deform and distort the facts we want to convey. Quickly we can become entrenched in our systems rather than in the message we need to share. Sometimes we have been intellectually arrogant and sometimes technically careless. Sometimes we become full of the world around us like a sponge and do not realize that we have been spiritually invaded. Then we try to "Christianize" and make theologically acceptable what is "adversary." This makes the authentic Christian life weak or makes it necessary to manage it, inserting the stewardship message into our own systems. Then we insist on doing what we can see and touch rather than what God promises and gives.

When we have small successes, we easily mistake our ways for God's. Then we have a confusing mixture of the Word and cultural trappings; and we have stewardship respectability with roots in the flesh, and we use God's resources to build earthly monuments. This is how it is possible to sustain materialism, covetousness, and greed under the protection of the church and in the name of God. The god that failed is man, confusing humanitarianism with Biblical stewardship. We congratulate ourselves and praise God for the "big bucks" we obtained from another big drive. Because these "big bucks" campaigns allow the church and most of its members to continue their earthbound slaveries without internal change and growth, we should not be surprised if God gives us a big "Whammy!"

The Scriptures ask us to commit ourselves to God and to His truth, not to the church as an organization. They do not appeal to reason or pragmatism, but plead for a growing relationship with Jesus Christ through repentance and forgiveness. That kind of stewardship is as much a relationship as an action.

CHAPTER SIX

DYNAMICS OF CREATIVE SPIRITUAL LEADERSHIP

People are as they are led. Paul teaches us much about the leadership qualities required for a church out on the firing line. The focus was always on the message, not the messengers; on the Treasure, not the earthen vessel carrying it. Paul was rather transparent, so that others could see God more than him. As a leader He demonstrated love by affection, by teaching, by giving, by persistence, by concern, and by availability. Acts 20 shows four dimensions of his ministry:

1. Toward God: He was "serving the Lord with all humility" (v. 19).

2. Toward the Church: Paul "kept back nothing that was helpful" (v. 20) and he declared "the whole counsel of God" (v. 27), commending them "to God and to the word of His grace, which is able to build you up and give you an inheritance among all those who are sanctified" (v. 32). Renewal must come from the leadership, for you cannot teach what you are not. Leaders should not be slaves

of tradition, but should recognize a constant need for "de-programming" from their own culture and worldly habits.

3. Toward the Lost: ". . . testifying to Jews, and also to Greeks, repentance toward God and faith toward our Lord Jesus Christ" (v. 21). A leader is a herald of the Gospel.

4. Toward Himself: Paul sacrificed for the ministry, "But none of these things move me; nor do I count my life dear to myself, so that I may finish my race with joy, and the ministry which I received from the Lord Jesus, to testify to the Gospel of the grace of God. . . . Remember that for three years I did not cease to warn everyone night and day with tears" (vv. 24, 31). He showed that a leader must be right with God: "Take heed to yourself and to the doctrine. Continue in them, for in doing this you will save both yourself and those who hear you" (1 Tim. 4:16). "A bishop must be blameless, as a steward of God, not self-willed, not quick-tempered . . . self-controlled, holding fast the faithful Word as he has been taught, that he may be able, by sound doctrine, both to exhort and convict those who contradict" (Titus 1:7–9).

Styles and Philosophy of Leadership

As there is maintenance stewardship and supply-side stewardship, so there are two kinds of leadership—lording leadership or serving leadership. Lording leadership centers more on protecting the interests of the church and getting the job done by supervision and control. It exercises influence and power over others in order to accomplish the task. Serving leadership allows Christ to be the Head in spirit as well as in letter; leaders as well as members submit to the will of God. With a servant's heart they deal with all members. The primary goal is to build people in the faith and to have a community of love by edifying through the use of Law and Gospel.

Four Signs of Failure

Seven years ago a layman shared what he termed to be "four signals of failure," which we need to recognize:

1. Little or no reading or input.

2. No goals. Goals should be prioritized and kept in mind constantly. The goals are to function as the touchstone for every thought, decision, plan, or action.

3. Blame others. Too quickly we can rationalize about the people with whom we work and the culture in which we find ourselves and the situation which we face, and then blame them. God will qualify us for whatever task he assigns us.

4. Quit trying. Some leaders have not said it or told others: They may be going through their jobs routinely, but in their minds they have told themselves that no one can lead these people to victory. So they have little success. In reality, they have quit trying.

Do you as a leader recognize any of these symptoms? If so, you will want to deal with them directly and firmly.

Principles for Doing God's Work in God's Way

Dynamic leaders know where they are going, have a plan for getting there, and work wholeheartedly at it. They will be tough-minded in pursuing their purposes.

Leaders will have a vision for the future, plotting plans and strategies which grow out of the educational process. With a high sense of mission, they will not become frustrated over the inertia, unproductiveness, and unwillingness of some churches. They will not depend on radically new forms, structures, and programs to become more effective, for the solution is less complicated than that. It is found in a simple shift of emphasis.

Leaders will be flexible, recognizing open doors. Routines, settling in imperceptibly, have become traditions. Tradition blinds us to opportunity. It is easy to deteriorate from an organism into an organization, from mission to maintenance, from function to form, from leadership to bureaucracy, and from participation to "spectatoritis."

Leaders will make disciplers out of disciples. After studying various movements to discover their effectiveness, Kenneth Strachan concluded: "The success of any movement is in direct proportion to the success achieved in mobilizing and deploying its total membership in the continuous propagation of its beliefs."[1] An aggressive equipping program is required to accomplish this.

Leaders will be thorough, avoiding superficiality. There should be the kind of dedication to which Frederick Wentz refers: Church members need to view themselves as paratroopers dropped behind enemy lines on Monday with the expectation of making their way back to the supply depot on the following

Sunday.

A high premium will be put on faithfulness and a team spirit among leaders. Workers and leaders will not be ranked, but each will be kept in high esteem and all glory will be given to God for what every leader contributes.

Leaders will make certain that the congregation "is effective to the degree that: it is clear as to its own identity; its people are committed and equipped to function; it is welded together in fellowship; it is divinely energized; it controls harmful tendencies; its leadership function is strong; every effort is marshaled, directed, and coordinated in the intelligent, deliberate, strategic effort to accomplish God's purpose for it."[2]

Utilize Growth Principles

God's work is far too important for church leaders to allow their congregations to drift because of lack of a planning process. The church growth process, properly understood and conducted, proposes that the Word be used in a maximum way for maximum effect. It encourages an educational process which fosters growth of the Word in the lives of people, seeking a life-changing response.

Growth is the nature and functional quality of the Gospel: ". . . the gospel . . . is bringing forth fruit . . ." (Col. 1:5–6). Growth is characteristic of and essential to the church: ". . . equipping of the saints . . . edifying of the body of Christ, till we all come to the unity of the faith and the knowledge of the Son of God, to a perfect man, to the measure of the stature and fullness of Christ; that we should no longer be children . . . but . . . may grow up in all things into Him . . . from whom the whole body, joined and knit together by what every joint supplies, according to the effective working by which every part does its share, causes growth of the body for the edifying of itself in love" (Eph. 4:12–16).

It is God's will that individuals grow: ". . . desire the pure milk of the word, that you may grow thereby. . . . Grow in the grace and knowledge of our Lord and Savior Jesus Christ (1 Peter 2:2; 2 Peter 3:18). It is God's will that churches grow: "You also, as living stones, are being built up a spiritual house" (1 Peter 2:5); the Book of Acts is filled with examples of churches growing in quality and quantity. In Titus 1:5 Paul shows that there is to be growth by correction: ". . . set in order the things that are lacking" or ". . . amend what was defective" (RSV). The Corinthians were told that abundant reaping requires abundant sowing of the Word (2 Cor. 9:6). Paul expected growth: "I commend you to God and to the word of His grace, which is able to build you up . . ." (Acts 20:32).

Church growth and obedience is the work of the Spirit: "It is God who works in you both to will and to do for His good pleasure" (Phil. 2:13). But God will not do this without the human instrumentality of minds and mouths to proclaim His Word and to plan His work. That is why church growth principles of evaluating our present situation, setting challenging goals, and adopting effective strategies are so important.

It is not our responsibility to make the church grow, but to obey God. It's God's business to make the church grow, and if we obey God, He will take care of growth. It is unfortunate that there are some who misunderstood and misread these basic assumptions and principles of the church growth process to the extent that they believe that it is unbiblical and sectarian. My observations from conducting over 250 meetings in congregations and regions, most of them area seminars, in the past three years is that the same ones who find these church growth ideas faulty are the ones who fail to perceive the perversion of grace in maintenance and traditional stewardship practices. Those who find church growth principles threatening should realize that there is divine measurement: "I know . . . I know . . . I know . . ."(Rev. 2:2, 9, 13, 19; 3:1, 8, 15). We should make positive evaluations of *all* that we are doing. That is one of the purposes of church growth.

Church growth encourages bountiful planting of the Word in every spiritual field. C.F.W. Walther in the last century said: "*Through the Word* the church is born and founded (becoming); . . . it is maintained and expanded (growing); . . .it is renewed when perverted (renewing); . . . it wages battles victoriously (conquering)." The growth process measures the health of the church, makes faith projections, and adapts comprehensive plan. The church will benefit from such an exercise.

In Search of Excellence

Leaders can learn lessons from America's best-run companies as reported in the book *In Search of Excellence.*[3]

These are ideas that are known by successful leaders but not applied as they should be. Church leaders will benefit by reading *In Search of Excellence* to learn about success principles that apply to churches as well as business.

Excellence is never an accident, but the result of unrelenting insistence on the highest standards of performance. It requires expectancy and a spirit of mission. It is contagious and unleashes an impact which influences people, committees, activities, and programs. It is a spirit which stimulates and inspires towards solutions for apathy and inertia.

Excellence requires a constant state of self-discovery and discipline. The only things that evolve by themselves are disorder, friction, and malperformance.

Basic Principles of Success

Seeds of Greatness provides some excellent insights for success, which can be applied by Christian leaders. In these paragraphs we share only a few nuggets.

The author tells about what he learned from his grandmother: "Things don't matter as much as your attitude toward them. You always get out what you put in. Plant apple seeds and you get apple trees." "Seeds of Greatness are not dependent upon the gifted birth, the inherited bank account, the intellect, the skin-deep beauty, the race, the color or the status. The Seeds of Greatness are attitudes and beliefs."

"Life is a self-fulfilling prophecy; you won't necessarily get what you want in life, but in the long run you will usually get what you expect." "The good old days are here and now!" "Winners work at doing thing a majority of the population are not willing to do."

Some steps toward perseverance: "Do high priority work first." "Concentrate your time and energies on the 20% of your activities, contacts, and concepts that have proven most productive." "If you fail the first time, try again." "Always expect the unexpected." "Be honest and logical when you approach your problems." "Do more than you are asked and contribute more than is required."[4]

Discipling

Jesus told us in the Great Commission: "Make disciples!" A disciple is a Christian who is learning, growing, maturing, and being shaped in the image of Jesus Christ, keeping strong to edify fellow Christians and to evangelize non-Christians. A disciple is a learner of God's Word who loves and trusts Christ, commits himself completely in service and obedience of faith, and knows and practices the truth.

Being a faithful disciple is not a natural matter nor acquired by reason, but by grace. It does not depend only on what we have received from Christ, but also on how we utilize these resources by our response and commitment. It does not take a talented person, but it takes all there is of him. A disciple is an overcomer, who faces problems and turns them into stepping-stones, and is victorious over the barriers set up by the devil, the world, and sinful flesh.

Jesus will not tolerate a compromising attitude on the part of His disciples, even when He teaches difficult lessons. Consider the time when many of His disciples heard Him and responded, "This is a hard saying; who can understand it?" (John 6:60 ff.). After a further explanation, we are told that "from that time many of His disciples went back and walked with Him no more." That's how hard it was. Peter expressed the truth when in answer to Christ's question, "Do you also want to go away?" He said, "Lord, to whom shall we go? You have the words of eternal life." Jesus knew that discipleship will never be easy or comfortable, but He gives blessings and privileges far outweighing the barriers and the crosses. Christ's disciples have His constant assurance that He will keep them in His care as they put their trust in Him alone.

A disciple renounces self, sets aside his own goals and ambitions in life as schedules, attitudes, and habits are changed. He acknowledges Christ not only as Savior but also as Master to be obeyed. The disciple will not be double-minded (James 1:6 – 8; 4:8). Rather, the goal of every dedicated disciple of Christ is to be "like his teacher" (Luke 6:40).

Jesus said that anyone who desires to go with Him must deny himself, take up his cross daily, and follow Him. If he does not do so, he cannot be His disciple. Jesus adds: "Whoever desires to save his life will lose it, but whoever loses his life for My sake will save it" (Luke 9:24). He makes an even stronger demand: "If anyone comes to Me and does not hate his father and mother, wife and children, brothers and sisters, yes, and his own life also, he cannot be My disciple" (Luke 14:26). Obviously, He is not recommending that we hate, but that we live by proper priorities. Jesus is to be our first priority always.

The disciple is willing to pay any price to have the will of God fulfilled in His life. He has a servant heart, not having an independent spirit but a deep love for people. He learns to discipline his life, putting no confidence in the flesh.

We seek faithful disciples who teach others in a multiplication process. Dawson Trotman, who reminded the church of its discipling responsibility, said: "Activity is no substitute for production. Production is no substitute for reproduction." Going to church meetings and talking about evangelism is not sufficient, but we are to go out evangelizing. The task is not to be performed by just a few people who produce much, but they are to train others, thus reproducing themselves and gaining many more active members. Every activity and organization should be an avenue for building and multiplying believers. Every new convert is to be discipled immediately and assigned to a discipler. Pastors, elders, deacons, and other leaders must set the pace.

The four stages of discipling are (1) the disciple evangelizes; (2) the convert is established in faith; (3) the new Christian is equipped and discipled as a disciple; (4) the new Christian becomes a discipler.

Steps to Becoming a Faithful Disciple

Leaders will make sure that people know that God has a plan for them, will help them see what God's methods have been, help them find their spiritual gifts and function within the body of Christ, and help them see the task before them. Leaders will show them how to sow the Word and help them bathe the entire process in prayer. Training focuses on what a World Christian is and how to have a Biblical life-style and body-action. Effective organization and support structures are developed.

There are a number of excellent books on discipling. *The Lost Art of Disciple Making,* by Leroy Eims (Zondervan/Navpress), is a good one for a starter.

Suggested Lessons to Teach

A minimum of 21 hours may be required for adequate disciple training, and possibly as many as 30 or more hours. A concentrated period of time is required, and each session should be at least three hours long. Several approaches can be considered: a session each week, possibly several each week, or two long weekends in a retreat setting. This training should tell the participant why, show him how to get started, and how to keep going. It should teach him to reproduce (teach others). The Biblical basis is 2 Tim. 2:2: "The things that you have heard . . . among many witnesses, commit these to faithful men who will be able to teach others also."

Basic topics to be studied, each having a varying length of consideration, are the following:

1. Who am I? Old Man-New Man, repentance-forgiveness, Vine and branches, God's workmanship, instruments of righteousness, managers. Source: *The Radical Nature of Christianity,* Waldo J. Werning.[5]

2. Who is God? Triune God, God of justice and love, Law and Gospel, grace, justification. (*The Radical Nature of Christianity,* chs. 4 and 5.)

3. The nature and function of the disciple (the kind of person God uses): Use some of the above materials.

4. How to study the Bible and teach it. In Bible study, try to find: a promise to claim and believe, an error to avoid or a sin to forsake, praise to give God or a prayer to ask Him for something, a command to obey in faith. (*The Radical Nature of Christianity,* ch. 7.)

5. Growth in knowledge, faith, love, and action. A life of trust. Understanding personal decision and involvement and incorporation.

6. Prayer and prayer life.

7. Body of Christ benefits, edifying and ministry. (*The Radical Nature of Christianity,* ch. 6 and 8.)

8. Maintain authority under Christ in leadership development and government. Produce responsible leaders in family and church. The "umbrella of protection" under grace: Eph. 5:1–2, 20–27; 6:1 (God, Christ, church, ministry, father-teacher, mothers, children); need for love (John 15:12), nourishment (1 Peter

2:2; Matt. 4:4), protection (1 Peter 5:8), training, discipline, bringing to maturity (Col. 1:28; Eph. 4:13).

9. Put spiritual things first and adopt priorities in earthly and physical matters (Mt. 6:19–33). Freed *from* the devil, world, and sinful flesh, and freed *to* serve, witness, give. True Christian freedom in relation to bondage to Christ.

10. Discovery and use of spiritual gifts.

11. Worldwide challenge as World Christians: committed to Christ, to Christ's body, to Christ's world (Acts 1:8).[6]

12. Live by God's promises, not by demands of the Law. Blessed to be a blessing (Gen. 12:1–3; Gal. 3:6–9, 29; Phil. 4:19).

Other selected lessons from Navigators ("Design for Discipleship"), *Shepherdology* study outline and cassettes by John MacArthur, Jr.

CHAPTER SEVEN
THE BEST WE CAN GIVE

God has never been satisfied with the "let's pretend" attitude regarding problems and easy solutions. Many laymen and pastors have told us that they are tired of the "tippy-toe" and the "let's take it easy" approach. This is not just a skirmish. It's war, one that needs to be fought by us, not the next generation. We do not have time to mark time or end the 20th century with a maintenance or holding action. We don't have 10 years. We have only now!

The songwriter challenges us: "Each age its solemn task may claim but once; make each one nobler, stronger than the last."[1]

To which we say, "The best we can give in our day is the Gospel." Follow in the footsteps of Paul: "For if I preach the gospel, I have nothing to boast of, for necessity is laid upon me; yes, woe is me if I do not preach the gospel!" (1 Cor. 9:16). We have been "entrusted with the gospel" (1 Thess. 2:4). This is the best we can give in our day.

We have not been called to reign in utopia, but to share the Word regularly in very messy situations. We dare not panic or react hastily to challenging situations. We need solid structure, clear vision, good teamwork, effective working models, strong guidance through problems and crises, and above all, complete commitment to the Word and will of God.

A ship's successful arrival in port is no accident. Good helmsmanship is necessary to gain our Gospel goals. There is a good chance that the readers of this book are the helmsmen God has set in the church. A ship can take almost any sea as long as it has power and the steering is in good shape. The most dangerous situation for a ship is to be dead in the water. The church is that spiritual ship, and the leaders the helmsmen. We will steer in the right direction not by sight (because sometimes it is absolutely dark), but by the trusted equipment and tools designed and supplied by God.

If our church's mission is controlled only by the traditional model, things will be out of control. Many of the steering problems come from poor theological and mission keels. Poor spiritual design makes it difficult to steer the church. Doubt makes us keep the ship at the dock or close to shore.

Supply-Side Stewardship has addressed itself to important phases of steering the church. The mission purpose, or plotting the port of destination, is the determining vision. Reaching that destination is possible through putting a team together on the basis of spiritual gifts. A working model has been suggested, one which works in practical situations—the educational process. The book also provides insights into the way the church can be steered through rough seas, problems.

It is frightening to be on a ship where there is poor helmsmanship and where the team is not prepared or committed to the task. Church leaders are called to steer people in the direction God wants them to move, and help them to stay on course. The helmsmen will aid people in giving the best they can.

The World in Which We Live

Many voices clamor to be heard, and many leaders ask for followers: The forces that pull us are philosophies, ideas, politics, materialism, religious compromises. At home we find a mad struggle for self-pleasure, and the media says by inference, "How can you be so stupid as not to purchase and enjoy our product? Don't deny yourself something which is your right." Abroad there are nationalism, religious bigotry, witch doctors, communism.

What about us Christians? God is asking very few to die for sharing His love. Most are afraid to die to self, which will bring greater joy to their lives, although they do not know or believe it.

Everywhere people are seeking, seeking, seeking, but they do not find security and satisfaction. They are real people. They hunger, they hurt, they aspire, they desire, they laugh, they cry, they die. Over three-fourths of them do not confess Jesus Christ as Savior and Lord.

This is the world in which we live and to which we have been called.

Crisis for Christianity

Thank God that we have growing spirituality and growing missions. But the percentage of those is so small. At home and abroad we find termites eating at the foundations of societies that once were stable. Families have been disintegrating at an alarming rate. Divorce, which God hates, is continuing to rise.

While many doors are open, some are closed to Christianity. It is time to abandon "little plans programs" and to organize around the Great Commission. Do we understand the Great Commission related to our local responsibilities? Have we caught God's signals?

A Sacred Responsibility Put on Us

Paul told us that we are entrusted with the Gospel and that a sacred responsibility has been put on us. Jesus said that we are the salt of the earth and the light of the world. Peter wrote that we are priests to show forth the praises of God. Do we act that way? In 2 Tim. 2 there are various metaphors related to who we are: soldier, athlete, farmer, worker, vessel for honor, servant. We spent an entire chapter on how each of us is to be a servant of Christ. A sacred responsibility has been laid on us to act that way. It is the best we can give. This means that we Gospelize (preach, tell, reach), educate, help, and heal.

If there is any lingering doubt as to the central task to which Christ calls His people, it should be dispelled by an inquiry into the final commandment of Christ and the result of obedience to that command on the part of believers. Perhaps no single passage of Scripture is more widely used to challenge Christians to faithfulness. Yet the majority of Christians are practicing it very poorly. Nevertheless, the best they can give is to be obedient to the Great Commission, which will revolutionize their lives.

In the Great Commission it is important to recognize that the One who speaks is the Risen Christ to whom all authority has been given and that the power for action comes from the Holy

Spirit. The "go" is a participle, not an imperative, and it should probably be translated, "as you go." "Make disciples" is the sole imperative and the central activity indicated in the Great Commission. These disciples will do the will of their Master. "All nations" is everybody. They are to be baptized in Christ's name. They are to be taught to observe all things He has commanded. They are to recognize that they do not go alone: "Lo, I am with you always, even to the end of the age."

The Great Commission is obeyed when Christ has first place, the Body functions together, builders build properly, and quality material is used. Then unity and oneness will be experienced in homes and churches, the sheep will follow the Shepherd, and the branches will abide in the Vine.

Responsibility for Church Leaders

The emergence of a strong and growing church means an awareness of the existence of unreached people: the inactives within the church, those who have heard but not responded, and those who have never heard. Dr. Win Arn has produced the "Church Growth Development Scale," which is designed to help leaders understand the process of change and to move their church forward.[2] We have revised and adapted it for the purposes of this book.

Move Your Church Forward on the Growth Scale

GROWTH DEVELOPMENT SCALE: 1. IGNORANCE; 2. INFORMATION; 3. INFUSION; 4. INDIVIDUAL CHANGE; 5. ORGANIZATIONAL CHANGE; 6. UNEASY APPLICATION; 7. INTEGRATION; 8. INNOVATION.

1. IGNORANCE: The congregation and leaders are uninformed of the mandate to make disciples. Committees/Boards have no unified direction or sense of mission. The congregation tends to be self-centered and self-serving. There is a total "maintenance" mentality and model as the people respond only to crises. They deal more with personalities than with issues. There is general disobedience to the Great Commission.

2. INFORMATION: There is general interest in learning more. Some questions are raised about more and better activities, yet there is general indifference and apathy toward the Great Commission. The "we-they" mentality is revealed in attitudes

toward the leaders and toward the church at large. HOW TO MOVE FORWARD FROM 1 TO 2: Study growth books in board/committee meetings. Give information and emphasize growth in sermons and Bible study.

3. INFUSION: There will be penetration of new ideas into the *status quo* to confront apathy, tradition, inertia, ignorance, and prejudice. A tendency to focus on problems more than solutions is still found. "Dreams" and goals are not yet in evidence. HOW TO MOVE FORWARD FROM 2 TO 3: Formulate a "dream" or goals. Sponsor growth meetings or seminars. Expand reading and study. Gain support from more leaders.

4. INDIVIDUAL CHANGE: It will be obvious now that some leaders and members have growth understanding and insights, catching a vision and ready to move forward. There will be a growing number of questions and comments about whether the present church activities are adequate. However, there will as yet be little support or reinforcement from the congregation for leaders or members who advocate change and growth ideas. HOW TO MOVE FORWARD FROM 3 TO 4: Make an evaluation of the total church and each of its tasks and board/committee assignments. Raise questions and issues regarding response to weaknesses and strengths discovered in the analysis. Give high visibility to the church's "dream" and goals. Seek public commitment to growth by leaders. Conduct a survey to identify areas of need and opportunities for outreach. Conduct a mini-retreat or "spiritual banquet" for leaders and potential leaders. Conduct a training course (Bible study) in spiritual gifts.

5. CONGREGATION (ORGANIZATIONAL) CHANGE: New activities, ministries, and programs are introduced in response to a new understanding and a new focus. New committees and structures are formed. New church goals are formulated. A mission/ministry statement is adopted. HOW TO MOVE FORWARD FROM 4 TO 5: Involve members in setting growth goals. Keep the "dream" before the membership. Establish and adopt a comprehensive statement of purpose. Identify needed new tasks, roles, and groups. Get a growing number of members to participate in continuing education. Use proven methods ("The Master's Plan," "Stewardship Growth Series").

6. UNEASY APPLICATION: Some mistakes and some successes are experienced. The learning process becomes rapid.

There is need for additional resources and materials. Training becomes apparent. There is a growing eagerness and consciousness toward growth. You are no longer a maintenance congregation but have adopted "supply-side" stewardship. HOW TO MOVE FORWARD FROM 5 TO 6: Publicize successes and recognize growth leaders. Quickly recycle potential failures. Gain full commitment from all leaders.

7. INTEGRATION: There is a growing ease and comfort in understanding and application of growth principles. More refinement of previous changes is seen and new steps are taken. You experience a secondary wave of results and successes. A sense of accomplishment is enjoyed. The educational process and model is fully implemented; the congregation sees itself as an equipping and learning center. HOW TO MOVE FORWARD FROM 6 TO 7: Plan training courses for leaders, another retreat or mini-retreat or "spiritual banquet" for all leaders and potential leaders. Expand the number of ministries by reinforcing the spiritual gifts process.

8. INNOVATION: Significant results are achieved and growth begins to perpetuate itself. There is general obedience to the Great Commission of Jesus Christ. There is a broad base of involvement of members, and leadership is growing. Members are aware of being World Christians. The congregation becomes a deployment agency to send members into the community and world as loving and caring messengers of the Gospel. HOW TO MOVE FORWARD FROM 7 TO 8: Enlarge the "dream," gain more staff, disciple a maximum number of members and all new members. Celebrate God's grace and blessing. Start or support a new mission.

General factors in following these steps include this understanding: Growth requires moving from one step on the Scale to the next. Leaders may be at a different place on the Scale than members. Correct strategy for growth will vary, depending on where the church is presently located on the Scale.

Leaders change before organizations change. Leaders should not try to change organizational programs and structures prior to changing individuals.

As you consider the Growth Development Scale and the message of this book, how do you rate yourself and your congregation: maintenance or supply-side? Do you operate more with an institutional and maintenance viewpoint or with the grace and education viewpoint?

Try to determine where your congregation is on the Growth Scale. Then prayerfully make your education plan to lead the congregation up the Scale to faithful obedience to Christ's Great Commission.

Afraid of Giants?

At one time God's people of the Old Testament had to make a decision between supply-side or maintenance, freedom or slavery, faith or sight. Was it to be Canaan with milk and honey or Egypt with bread and slavery? When their representatives came back from Canaan, they reported a land of milk and honey—and of giants. Caleb and Joshua said: "Let us go up at once and take possession, for we are well able to overcome it" (Num. 13:30). The majority said: "We are not able to go up against the people, for they are stronger than we. . . . We saw the giants" (vv. 31, 33). Two leaders saw with the eyes of faith, the others by sight alone.

The people, afraid of the giants, wept and said they should have died, and they murmured against Moses and Aaron (14:1–2). They wanted to select a new leader and go back to slavery in Egypt (14:4). Gaining and managing God's supply scares some people. Freedom without rule books seems more difficult than bondage.

Joshua and Caleb reminded them: "If the Lord delights in us, then He will bring us into this land. . . . Only do not rebel against the Lord, nor fear the people of the land, for they are our bread. . . . The Lord is with us. Do not fear them" (v. 8–9).

There was an amazing response from those fearful and fretful folks: They shouted that Joshua and Caleb should be stoned (v. 10).

At that God's patience wore thin, and He said to Moses: "How long will these people reject Me? And how long will they not believe Me?" (v. 11). Moses pleaded for the people, reminding God of past deliverance and asking Him for mercy and forgiveness.

Regarding the rebels, God asked: "How long shall I bear with this evil congregation who murmur against Me?" (v. 27). The rebels had to wander for 40 years and die.

The account continues in the Book of Joshua, when God was ready to take His people into the Promised land. God said: "No man shall be able to stand before you. . . . Only be strong and very courageous, that you may observe to do according to all the Law which Moses My servant commanded you" (1:5, 7).

This was not just a divine pep-talk but bedrock assurance. Humanly speaking, there was no hope against the towering giants of Canaan. God's view, however, revealed that the battle had already been won, as it was fought in His strength and by His command: "Have I not commanded you? . . . Do not be afraid, nor be dismayed, for the Lord your God is with you wherever you go. . . . Command the people, saying, 'Prepare provisions for yourselves, for within three days you will cross over this Jordan, to go in to possess the land which the Lord your God is giving you to possess' " (1:9, 11).

The people said: "All that you command us we will do, and wherever you send us we will go" (1:16).

Several of our insurmountable challenges, our own Canaans, may be the maintenance model or the desire to gain every member of the congregation to be a Bible student. We know that God wants to give the victory, but we are afraid to move into the land. Forward to Canaan or back to Egypt? Shall we live from God's supply house or live under bondage in organizational maintenance?

Remember that it is the size of your God, not the size of your giants, that counts! Our God and His Word are faithful, trustworthy, never wrong in guidance. He is never in short supply with His provisions. He is never slack with His love. He has given us victory over the giants.

Do Something Drastic!

A number of years ago we led a mission tour group through Japan with a Buddhist guide. After viewing the effective work of one of our Christian day schools, he was highly impressed and made an impassioned speech to our group. He noted first of all that our devotions informed him that Christ not only died on the cross for the world, but that Christ died for him personally, for Taki. He said that he had associated with many groups who came to Japan, for whom he was guide. He had never observed anything like this, and he was impressed that we had something to share with Japan. He had only one thing more to share: He could not tell us what to do or how to do it, but he said, "Whatever you do, do something drastic!" A Buddhist challenge to Christians!

We cannot tell you what to do in your congregation. Ideas and plans have been offered in this book. You decide what should be done now. But whatever you do, do something drastic!

Go Boldly!

It is doubtful whether there is a better conclusion to this book than Heb. 4:16: "Let us therefore come boldly to the throne of grace, that we may obtain mercy and find grace to help in time of need."

Go boldly to the throne of grace for mercy: Follow the 12 spiritual steps with the use of Law and Gospel in order to keep fresh that we are completely and freely forgiven of all of our sins and that our guilt has been taken away. We are Christ's for time and for eternity. It has all been done for us. Seek it all, not just a part of it.

Go boldly to the throne of grace in time of need: Not just for personal problems in the spiritual and material realm, but also for needs in the body of Christ. Go boldly that God may give you grace to be a true servant, serving your family and loved ones, serving your congregation and community, serving your world. Go boldly to the throne of grace for other people's needs. Go boldly to do something beautiful for God.

Bold steps were taken to produce the beautiful Chapel of the Holy Cross of Sedona, Ariz., hewn out of the rocks on the side of a mountain. The artist wrote: "As an artist, this is my offering . . . 'Ad majorem Dei gloria' (To the greater glory of God) in answer to the One who in order to save us stretched out His arms on the cross . . . that the church may come to life in the souls of men and be a living reality. . . ."

Will you make your commitment with me: "As a _______ (worker, student, homemaker, whatever your vocation or occupation is), this is my offering to the greater glory of God, in answer to the One who in order to save me stretched out His arms on the cross."

May your servanthood and witness contribute, "that the church may come to life in the souls of men and be a living reality!"

Go boldly! Offer the best you can give!

APPENDIX A

CONGREGATION'S COMPOSITE FACTS AND STATISTICS

The evaluation, goal setting, and strategy planning of congregations depend on where they have been and where they are. Attention must be given to all aspects of the congregation, including membership and its intake and output. Training and leadership programs are vital.

We are offering you the "Composite Facts and Statistics of Congregations," which provides encouragement to keep records of the intake and output of congregations through their activities. It shows the people's general stewardship and expression of faith.

You will want to look into the records of your congregation for the past few years and then keep current records of the quality and quantity of its growth. This will help you uncover the strengths and weaknesses of your congregation.

CONGREGATION'S COMPOSITE FACTS AND STATISTICS

INTAKE AND OUTPUT - GENERAL STEWARDSHIP

GROWTH AND EXPRESSION OF FAITH

CONGREGATION AND ADDRESS: ______________________________

MEMBERSHIP	1984	1985	1986	1987	1988	1989	1990
Baptized							
Communicants							
Need referral to other congregations							
Number of delinquents							

INTAKE

A. Worship attendance (%)
B. Communion attendance (%)
C. Bible class (classes-attendees)

OUTPUT

Members active in evangelism calls
D. Abilities (members active in service)
E. All-purpose giving (per com.)
F. Missions (per com.)

TRAINING AND LEADERSHIP

G. Have a stewardship committee
H. Have an active stewardship program
I. Reached % of members in Every Member Contact for stewardship
J. Members making commitment
K. Mission education program
L. Personal money management program
M. Wills and estate planning program
N. Education on body and health
O. Used Financial Priorities instrument
P. Used Time and Talent Survey

(Identification codes on next page)

IDENTIFICATION CODES

A. Divide weekly worship attendance by baptized membership
B. Divide total at communion all year by communicant membership
C. All communicants attending all Bible classes, plus Sunday school teachers: Number of classes and attendees, i.e., 3–68
D. Total number of communicants active in service tasks or holding officer positions
E. Divide total income for all purposes by number of communicants
F. Divide World Mission (District and Synod) by number of communicants
G. Formal *stewardship* committee?
H. Conduct an actual program, not incidental activities
I. What percentage of members (families or units) were reached in an Every Member Contact (Group Meetings, Every Member Visits, Personal Interview, Cottage Meetings, or combination of several of these)?
J. How many members made commitments?
K. Supply year-round mission education
L. Provide information and materials to members on personal money management and financial planning
M. Provide information and encouragement for members to write wills and to plan estates and consider deferred gifts
N. Educate and encourage members to adopt good health habits
O. Finance committee and treasurer utilize "Financial Priorities" instrument to adopt annual budget (*Christian Stewards—Confronted and Committed,* pp. 182–84)
P. Used Time and Talent Enlistment sheet or form.

APPENDIX B
CONGREGATION'S ORGANIZATIONAL CHART COMMENTARY

Proceeding from the Trinity, the incarnate Christ has established His kingdom through local congregations with the office of the ministry and the function of the body of Christ (communion of saints, royal priesthood). The voting membership makes decisions and resolutions to express policies that flow from their responsibility in the kingdom of Christ in order to help carry out the ministry of the Gospel of Jesus Christ effectively. This is a structure designed to express spiritual authority according to Biblical injunctions, not a managerial structure.

Under the leadership of the pastor, the spiritual power structure is centered in the Board for Christian Discipleship (elders or deacons), where an elder serves as adviser to each committee or commission.

The pastor and his staff are attached both to the voting membership and to the Board for Christian Discipleship. The Council or Board of Directors are the managers of business affairs, but the pastor and elders are the spiritual heads of the congregation, who are represented on the Council or Board of Directors by the pastor and head elder.

The voting group calls the pastor, as well as elects the members of the Board for Christian Discipleship. However, the pastor retains the spiritual authority under Christ, but shares many responsibilities with the Board of Elders (Shepherds).

CONGREGATION'S ORGANIZATIONAL CHART

Triune God

Incarnate Christ

The Body of Christ
Communion of Saints
Royal Priesthood

Local Congregation

OFFICE OF MINISTRY
Pastor
&
Staff

Voting
Membership

Board for Christian Discipleship (Elders or Deacons)
(An elder serves as advisory on each commission)

COUNCIL OR
BOARD OF DIRECTORS
Chairman of Each Commission
President
VP
Sec'y
Treas.
Fin. Sec'y

Shepherds
&
Elders

Nurture
Education

Adults
Children
Teens
Day School

Evangelism
Church Planting

Stewardship

Special Ministry

Singles
Retirees

Social Ministries

Trustees

NOTES

Chapter One

1. Richard F. Lovelace, *Dynamics of Scriptural Life - An Evangelical Theology of Renewal* (Downers Grove, IL: Inter-Varsity Press, 1979), p. 75. Recommended for reading as additional resource.

2. Donald G. Bloesch, *Faith & Its Counterfeits* (Downers Grove, IL: Inter-Varsity Press, 1981).

3. John White, *The Golden Cow* (Downers Grove, IL: Inter-Varsity Press, 1979), p. 12. Recommended for reading as additional resource.

4. Ibid, pp. 20, 67, 70, 71, 75, 76, 79, 81, 82.

5. Adolph Koeberle, *The Quest for Holiness* (Minneapolis: Augsburg, 1938), p. 152.

Chapter Three

1. Lovelace, p. 101.

2. Ibid., p. 236.

3. Judson Cornwall, *Let Us Enjoy Forgiveness* (Old Tappan, NJ: Fleming H. Revell, 1978), p. 72.

4. Ibid, p. 159.

5. Koeberle, pp. 150 – 51.

6. *Twelve Steps and Twelve Traditions* (Alcoholics Anonymous World Services, Box 459, Grand Central Station, NY 10163), Table of Contents. Recommended for reading as additional resource.

7. John MacArthur, Jr., *Shepherdology* (Word of Grace, PO Box 4000, Panorama City, CA 91412).

8. *Trust Account Transfer* tracts and forms are available from the Stewardship Growth Center, 1914 Wendmere Lane, Fort Wayne, IN 46825.

Chapter Four

1. Michel Quoist, *The Christian Response* (Dublin, Gill & McMillian, 1965), p. 4.

2. Lyle E. Schaller, "Minister of Health," *Church Management—The Clergy Journal* (Jan. 1985), pp. 22 – 23.

3. David Chilton, *Productive Christians in an Age of Guilt Manipulators* (The Institute for Christian Economics, PO Box 6116, Tyler, TX 75711).

Chapter Five

1. The booklet *New Steps to Security and Happiness,* by Waldo J. Werning (Stewardship Growth Center), embodies a challenging message based on the 12 steps.

Chapter Six

1. W. Dayton Roberts, *Strachan of Costa Rica* (Grand Rapids: Eerdmans, 1971), p. 86.

2. Joe S. Ellis, *The Church on Purpose* (Cincinnati: Standard Publ., 1982), p. 16.

3. Thomas J. Peters, Robert H. Waterman, Jr., *In Search of Excellence* (NY: Warner Books, 1982), pp. 13 – 17. Copyright Harper and Row. Recommended for reading as additional resource.

4. Denis Waitley, *Seeds of Greatness* (NY: Pocket Books, Simon & Schuster, 1984), pp. 188 – 89, 214, 229 – 31. Recommended for reading as additional resource.

5. Waldo J. Werning, *The Radical Nature of Christianity* (Pasadena, CA: William Corey Library, 1975). Recommended for reading as an additional resource.

6. Werning, *Vision and Strategy for Church Growth* (Grand Rapids: Baher, 1983). Recommended for reading as additional resource.

Chapter Seven

1. Denis Wortman, in *Lutheran Worship*, Hymn 258, v. 1.

2. Dr. Win Arn, "Growth Report No. 5," *Church Growth* (709 E. Colorado, Suite 150, Pasadena, CA 91412). Recommended for subscription.